Sunflower

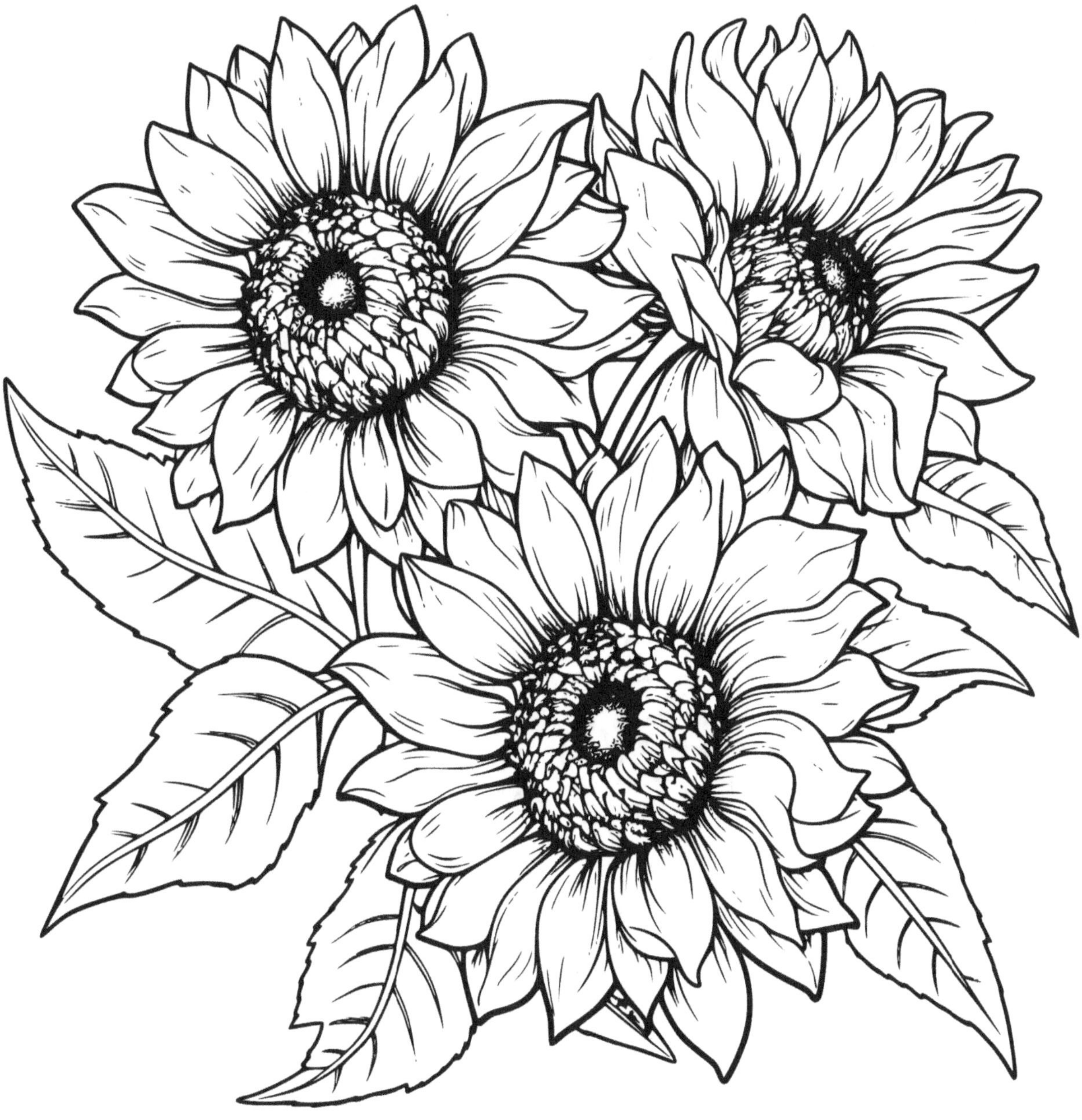

With its bright yellow petals, sunflowers symbolize adoration, loyalty, and longevity.

Bouquet

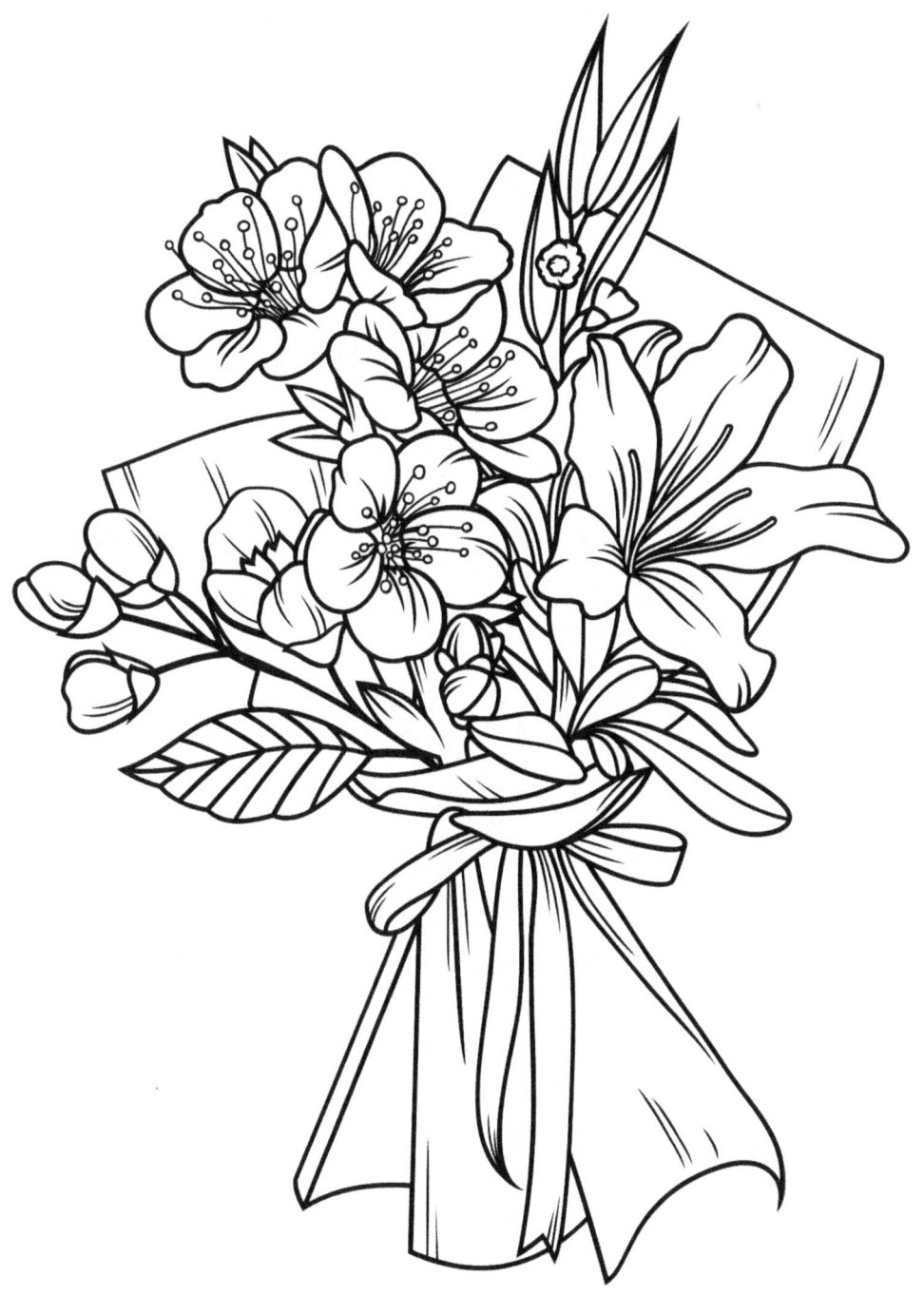

The history of the bouquet dates back to ancient times when flowers were gathered and arranged for both decorative purposes and symbolic meanings.

Daisy

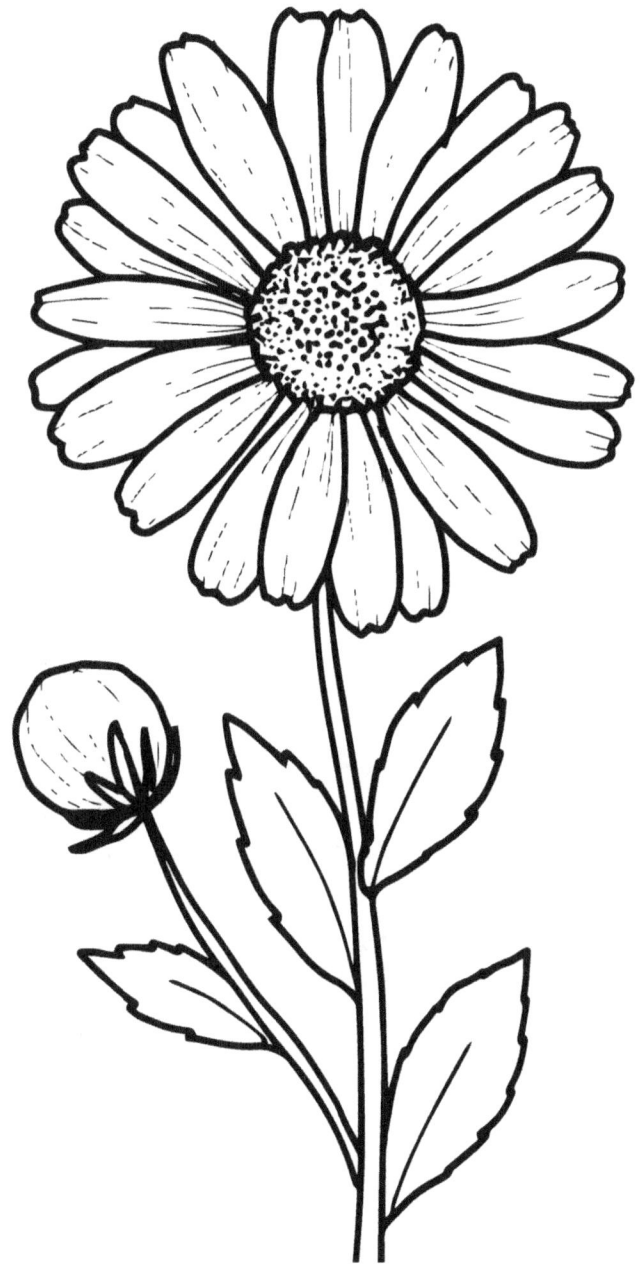

Simple and cheerful, daisies represent purity and innocence, making them a popular choice.

Rose

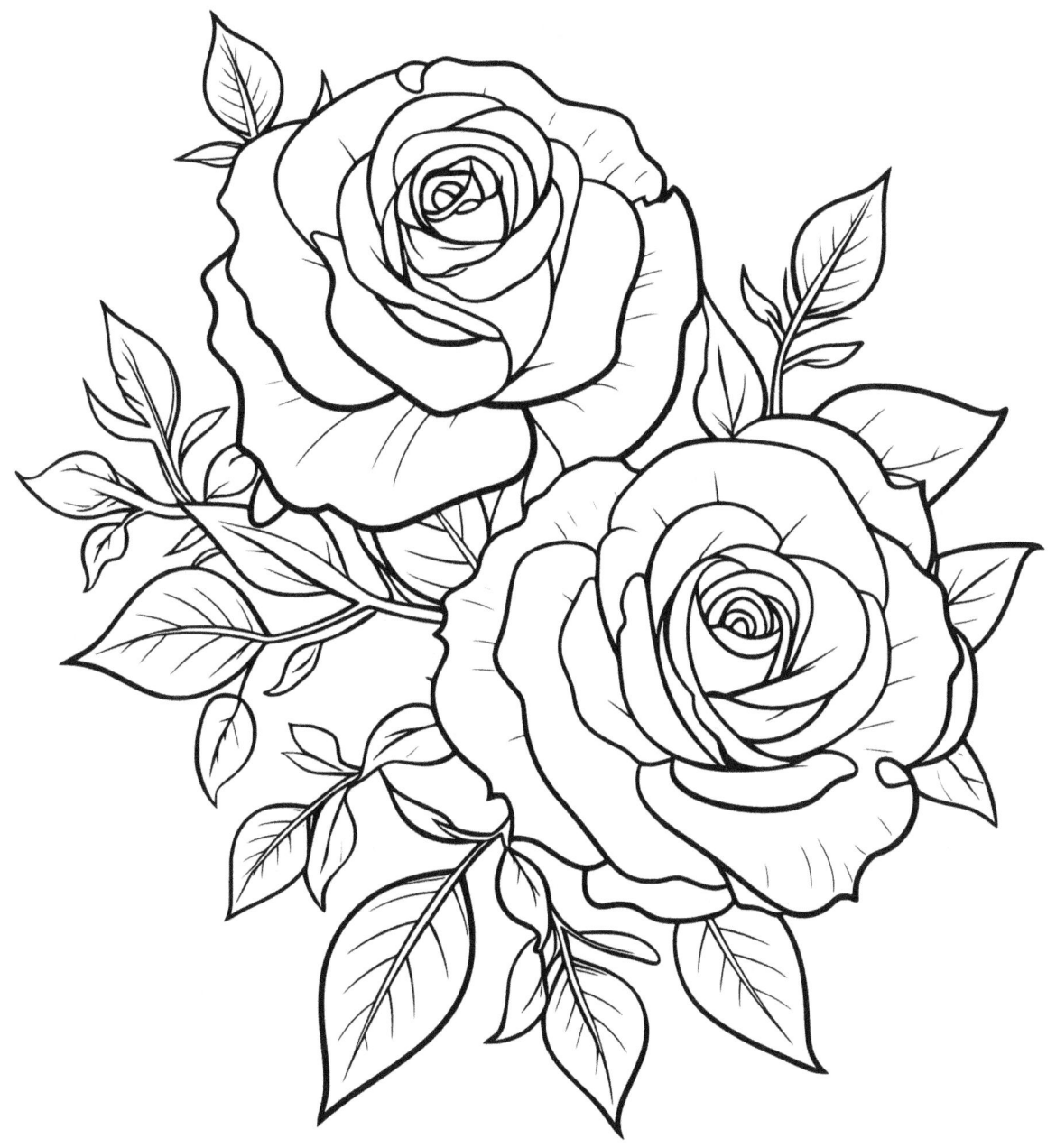

Known for its beauty and fragrance, roses come in various colors and are often used in bouquets.

Lily

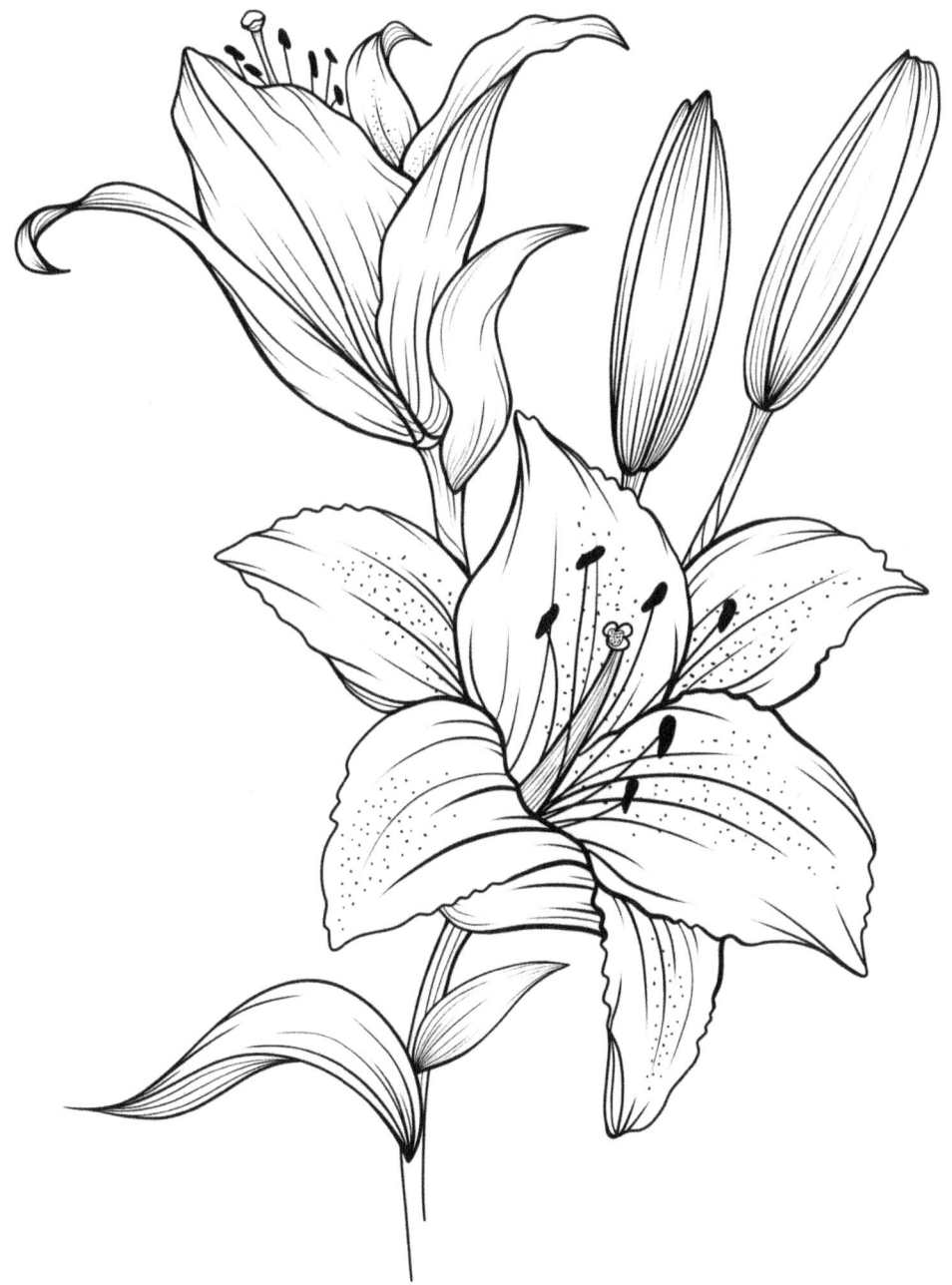

Graceful and fragrant, lilies are often associated with purity, renewal, and transition. They are highly toxic to cats.

Orchid

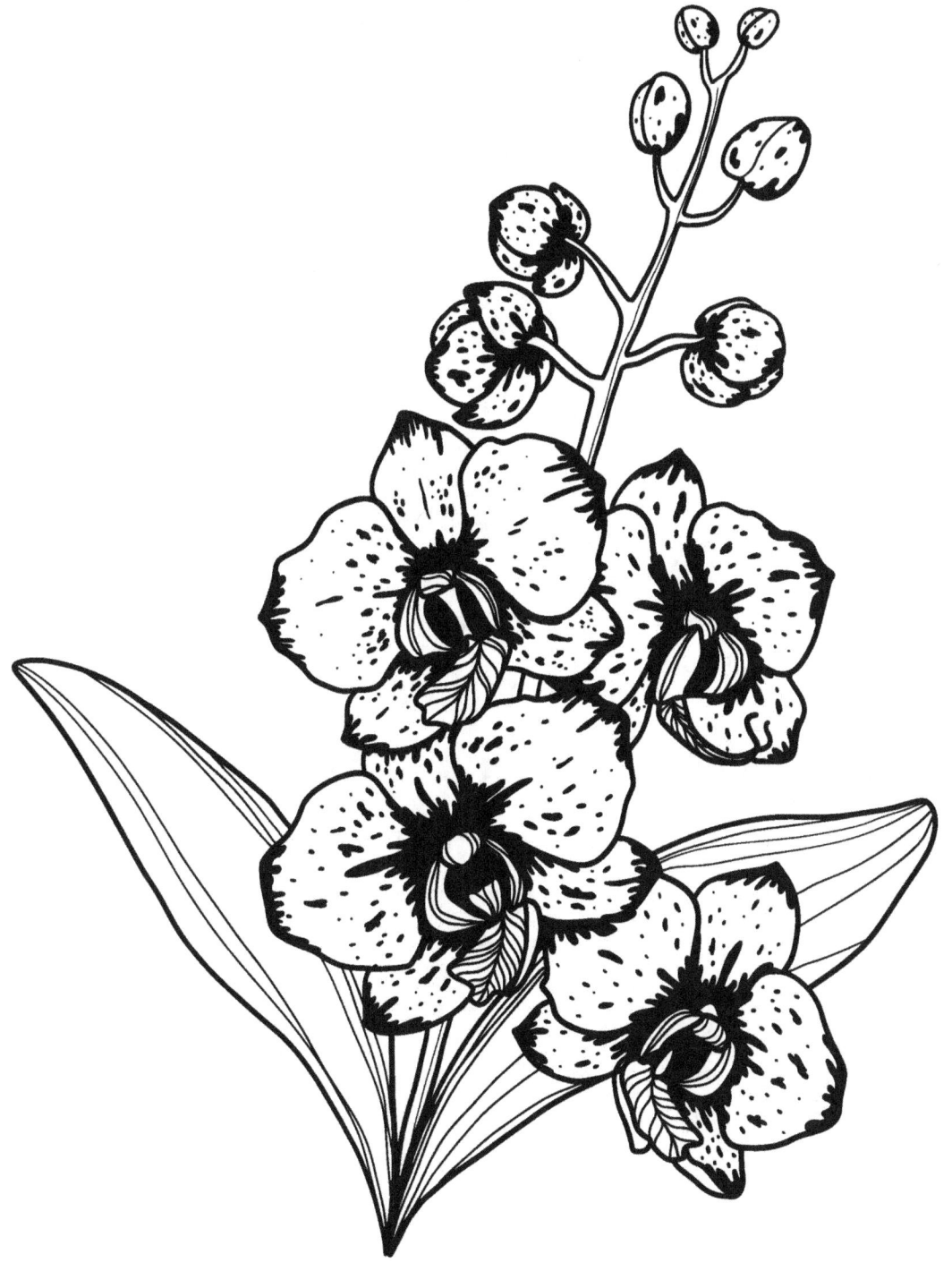

Exotic and elegant, orchids symbolize love, luxury, and beauty, making them prized flowers.

Peony

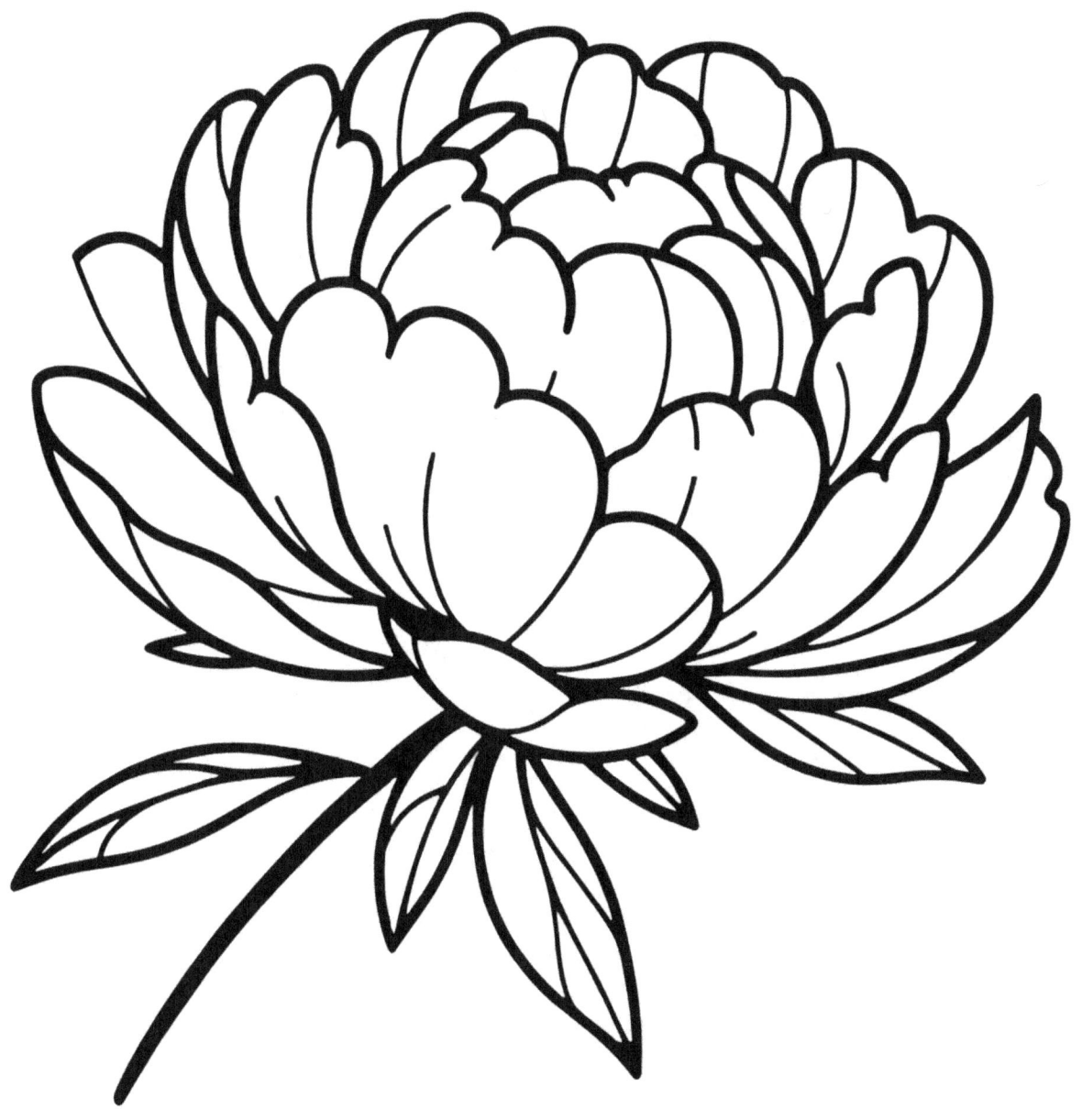

Large, lush, and fragrant, peonies symbolize romance, prosperity, and good fortune.

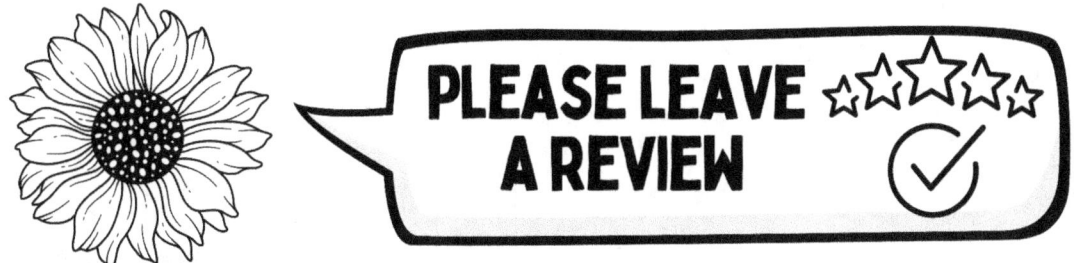

Thank you very much for purchasing my book. As a small indie publisher, it means a lot and I hope you find as much joy in coloring these beautiful horses as I did in creating them.

If you have 60 seconds, it would mean the world to me if you could leave a short review on Amazon, it does wonders for the book and I love hearing how you benefited from it.

TO LEAVE YOUR FEEDBACK

1. Open your camera app
2. Point your mobile device at the QR code below
3. The review page will appear in your web browser
4. Scroll down to the Customer Reviews Section

OR VISIT:

https://www.cascadiawavemedia.com/review.php?book=B0D2VK42QC

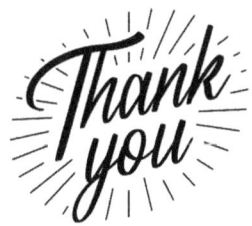

Hydrangea

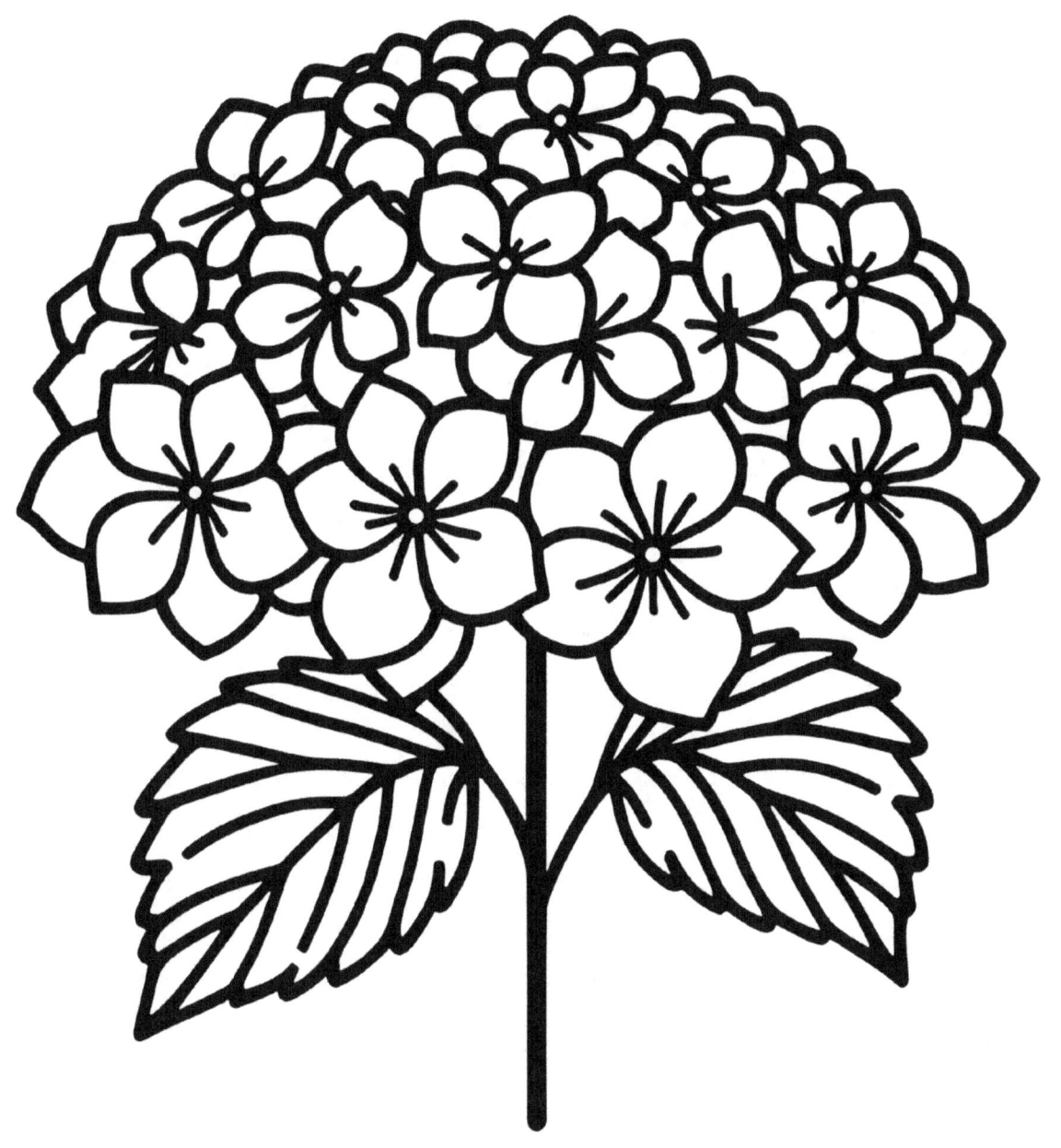

Hydrangeas are known for their large clusters of blooms and come in various colors.

Carnation

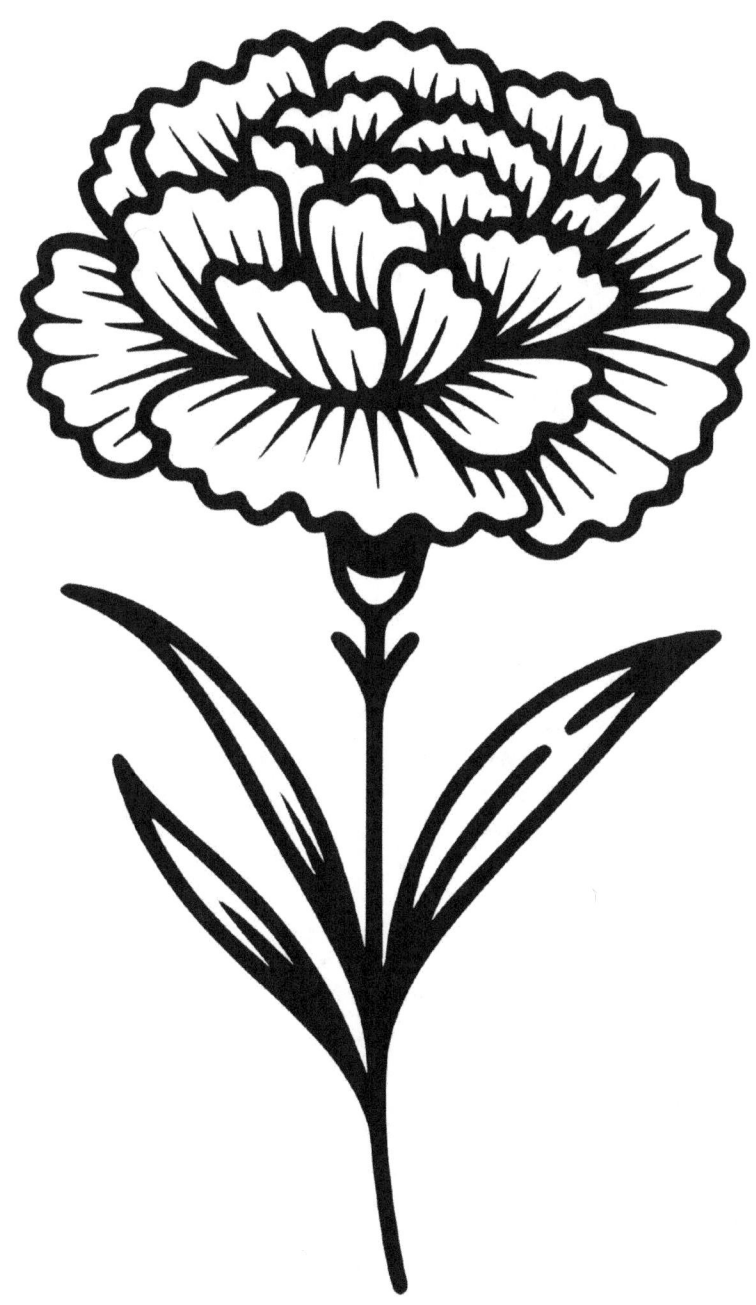

Carnations are versatile flowers with a wide range of colors and meanings, often used in bouquets.

Gerbera Daisy

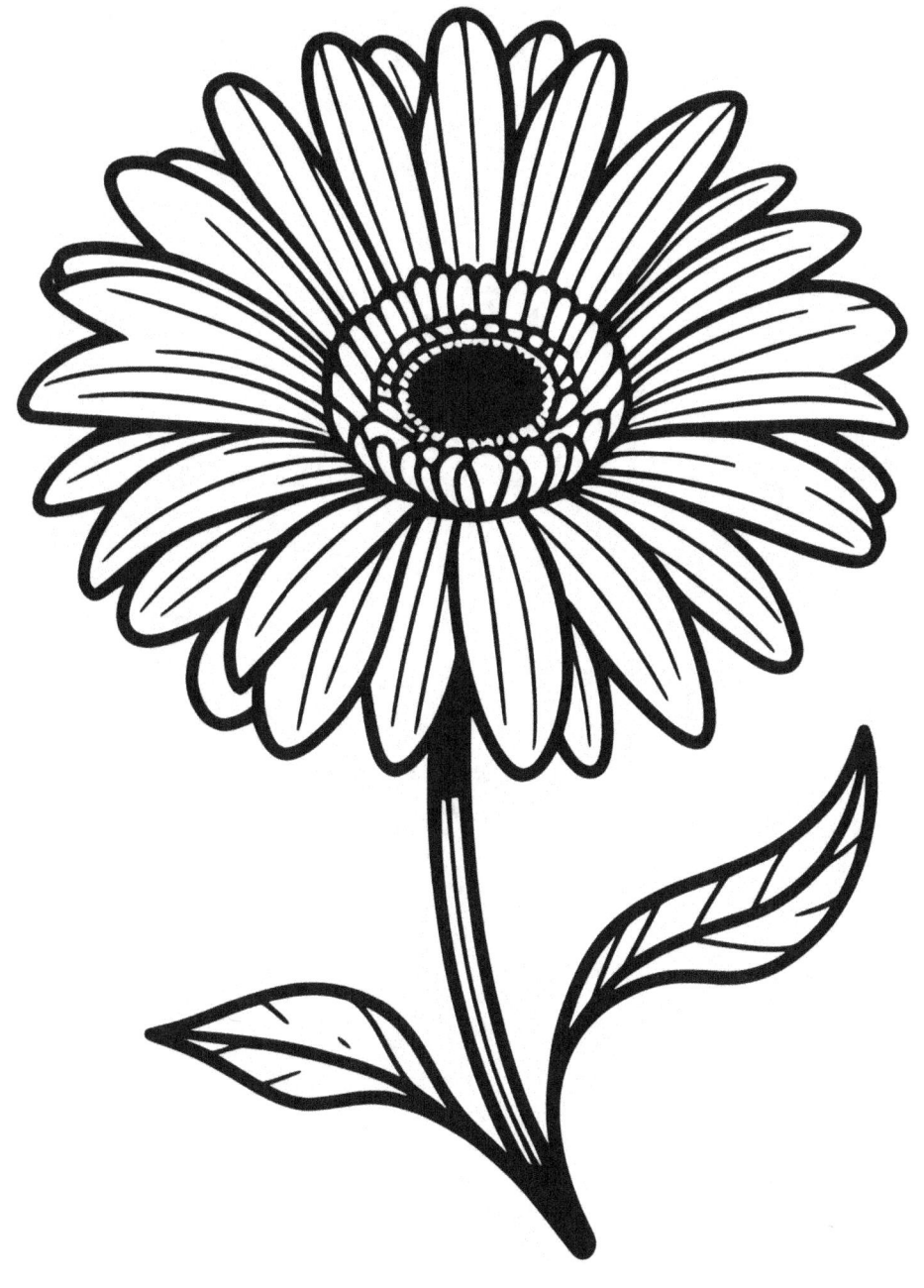

Vibrant and cheerful, gerbera daisies are popular for their bold colors and long vase life.

Iris

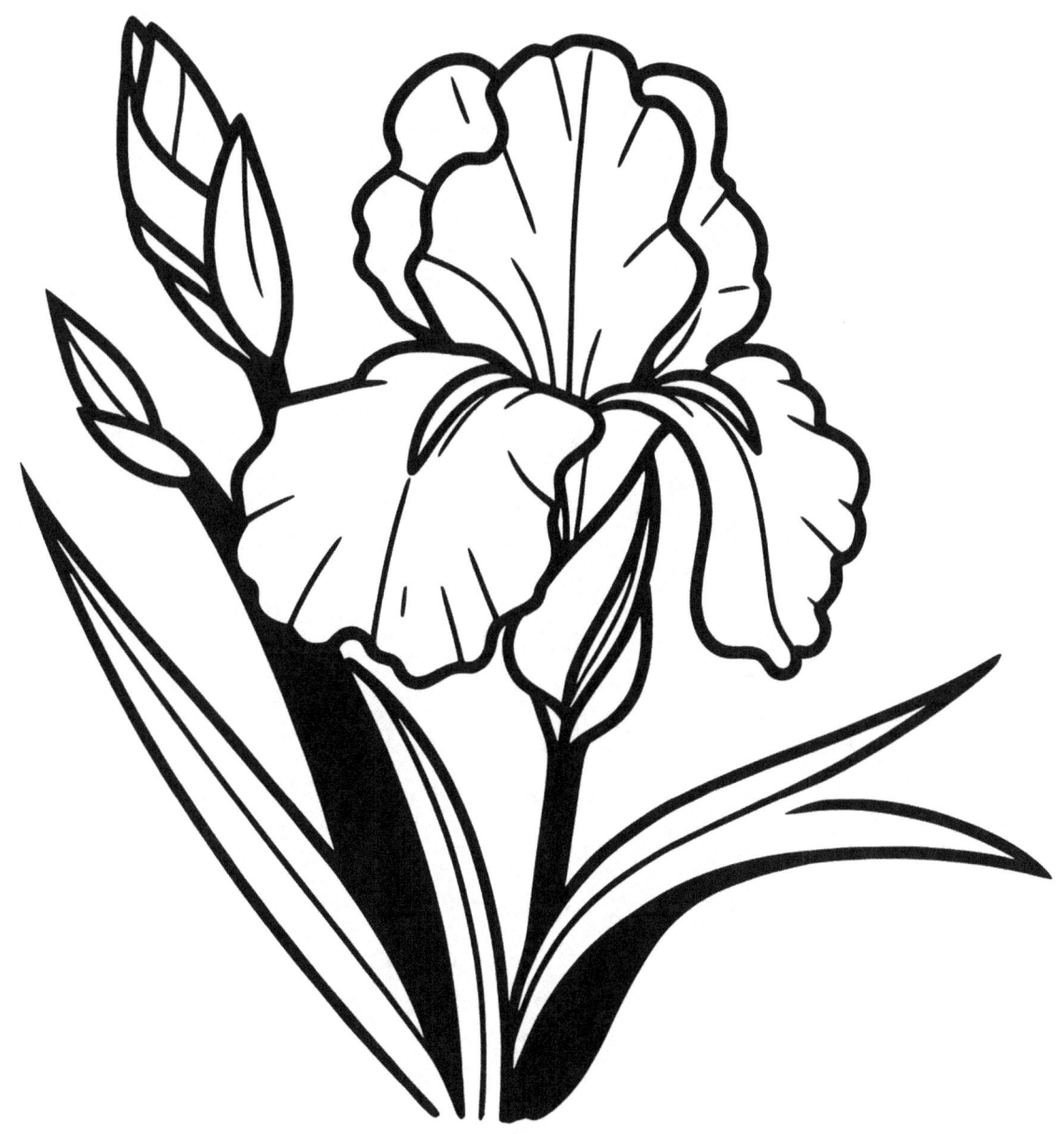

Iris flowers are distinctive with their unique shape and vibrant colors, symbolizing faith and wisdom.

Lavender

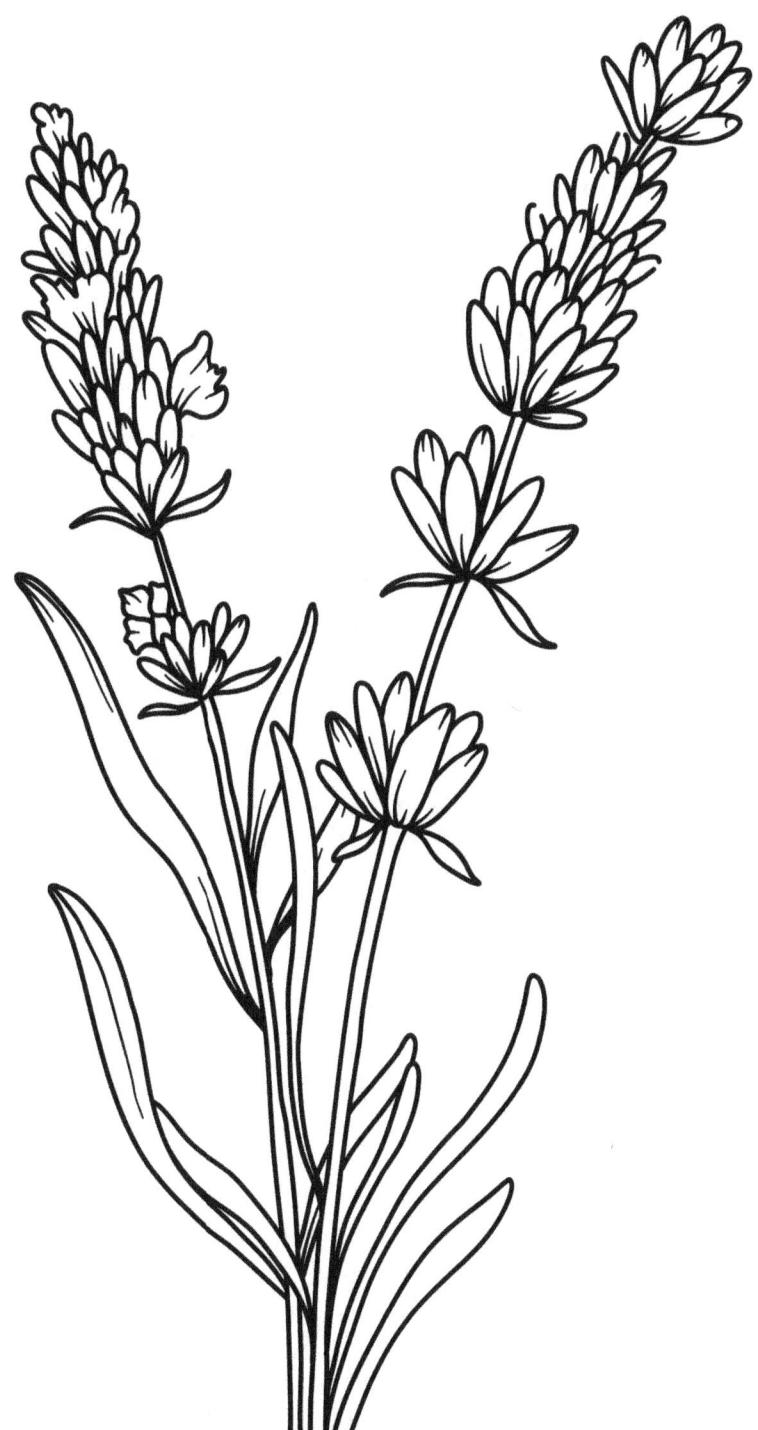

Fragrant and soothing, lavender is known for its calming properties and beautiful purple blooms.

Daffodil

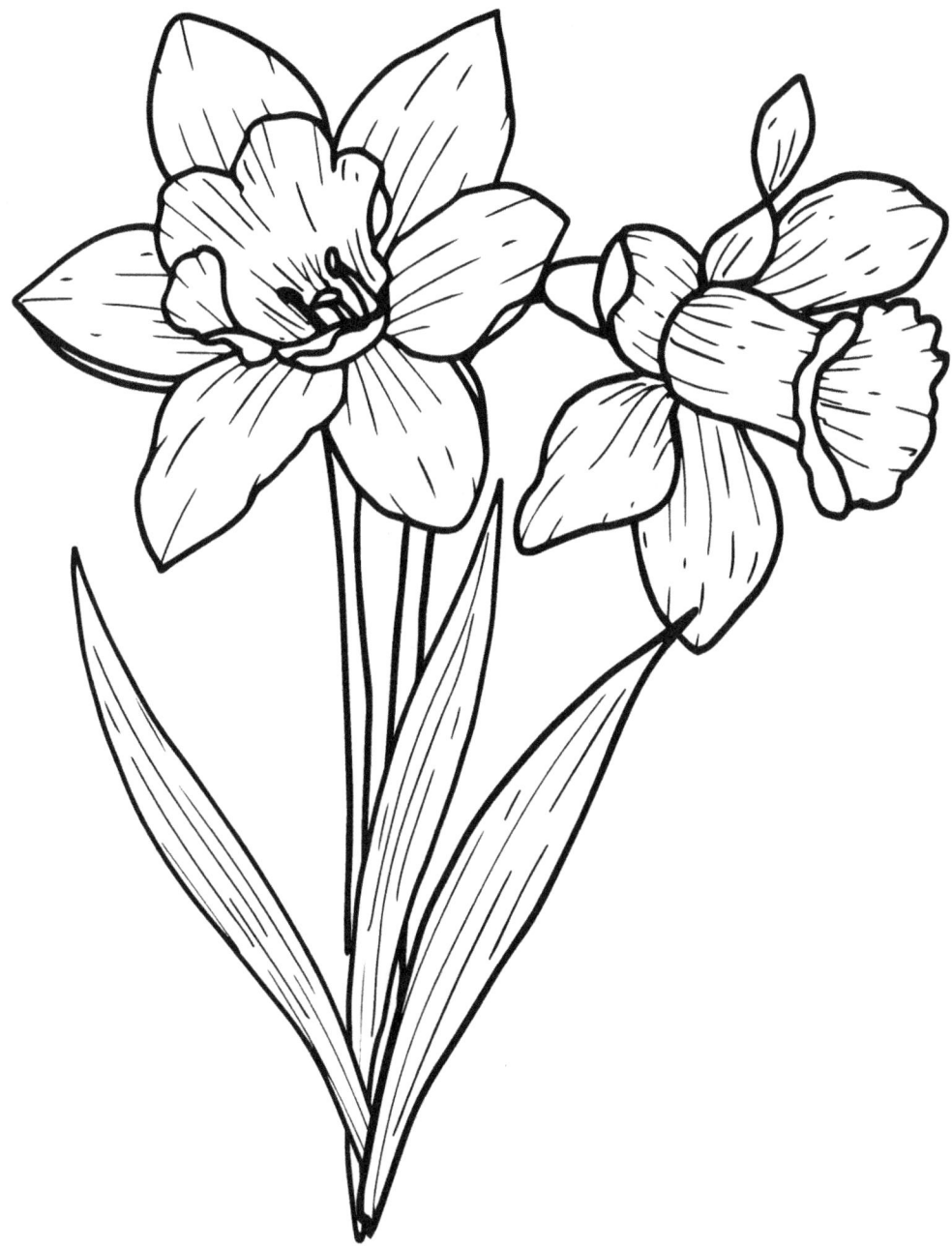

Daffodils, also known as narcissus, herald the arrival of spring with their cheerful yellow flowers.

Chrysanthemum

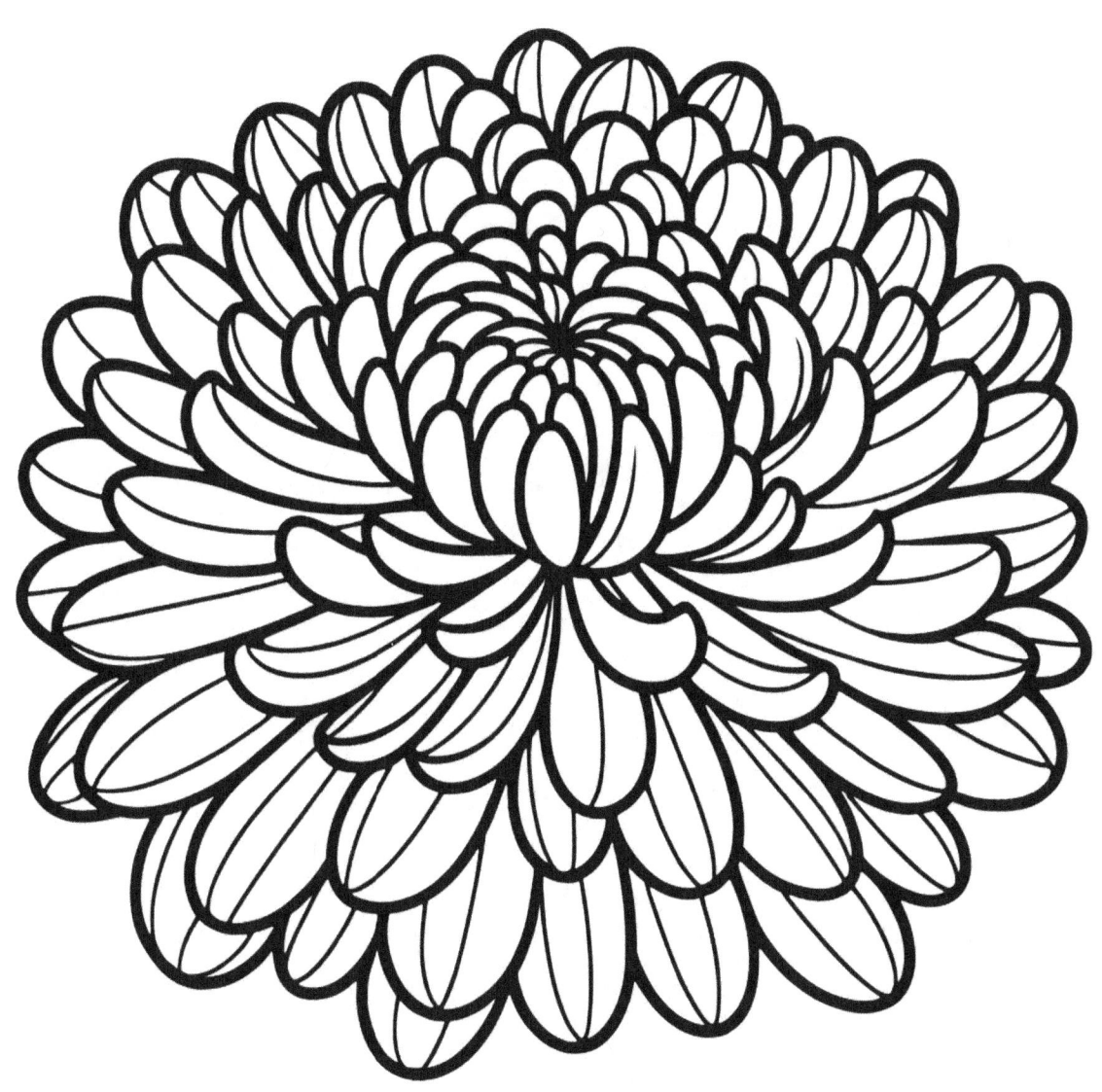

Chrysanthemums come in various colors and symbolize friendship, joy, and positivity.

Snapdragon

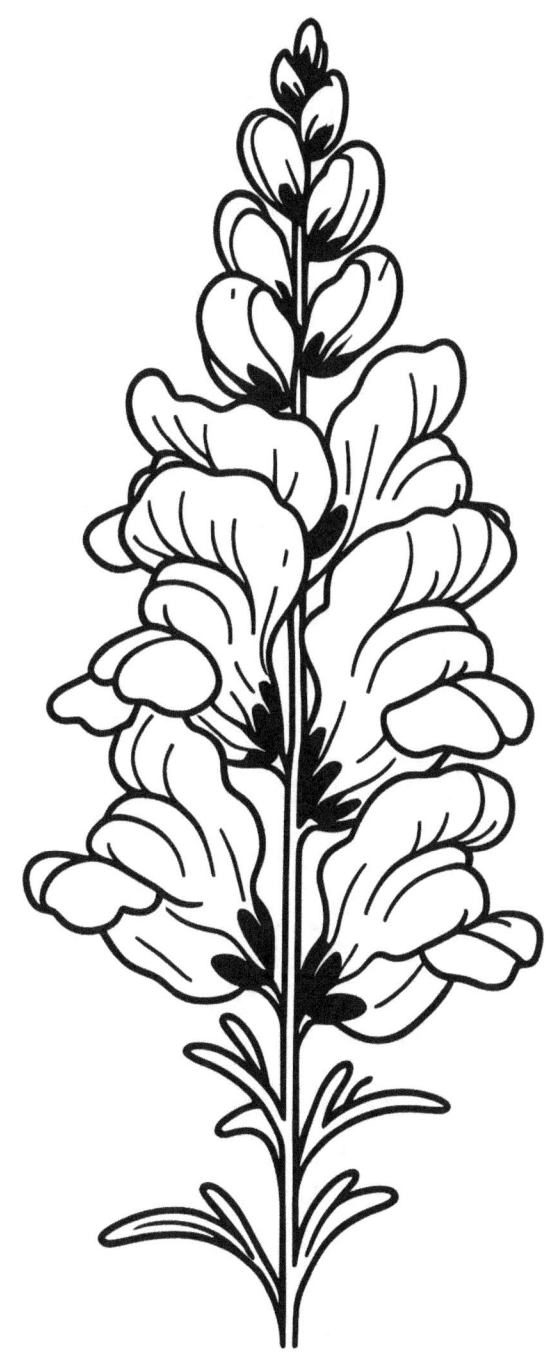

Snapdragon flowers have unique snap-like blooms and are often used as cut flowers in arrangements.

Marigold

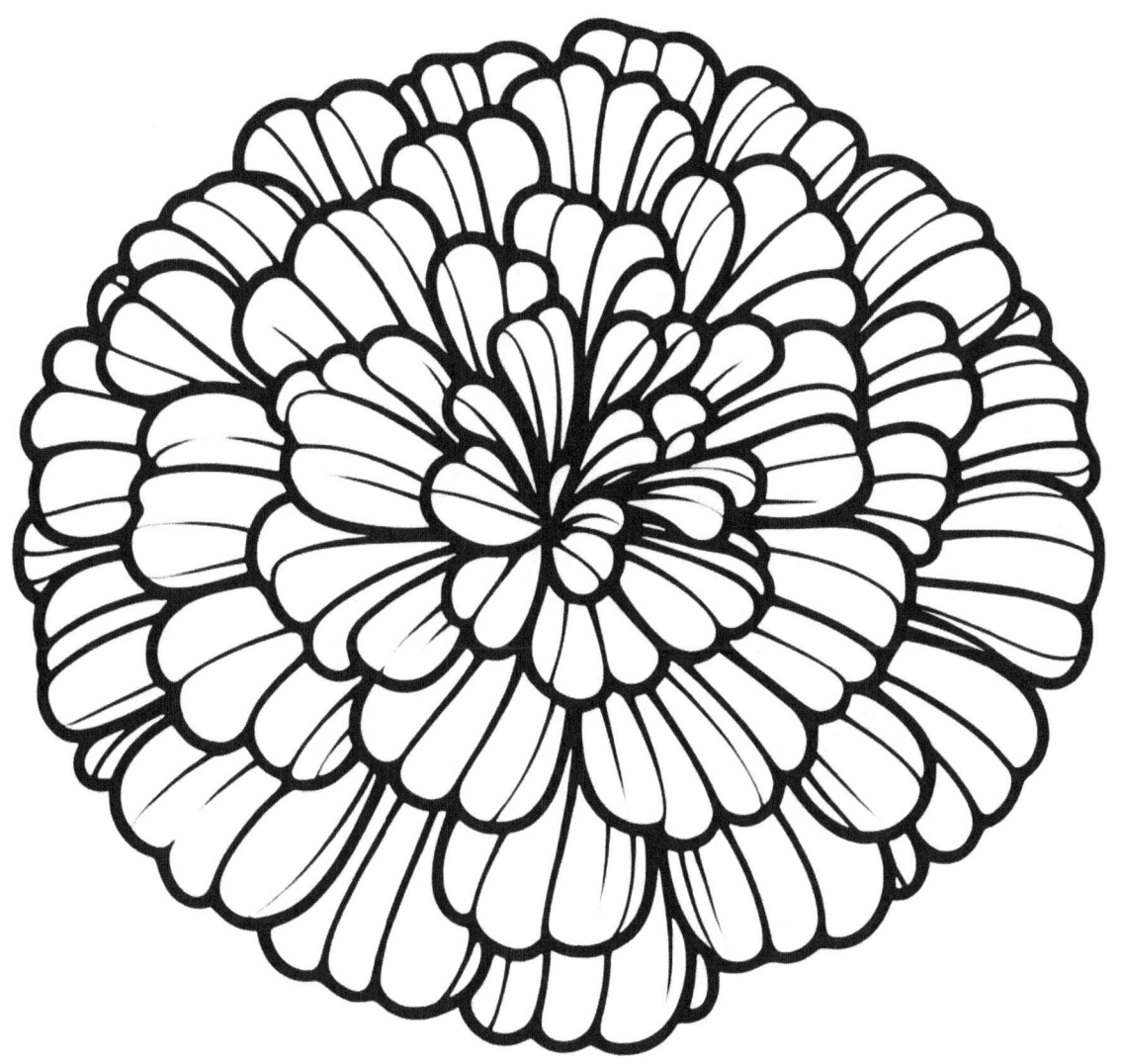

Marigolds are bright and cheerful flowers that symbolize optimism, joy, and success.

Tulip

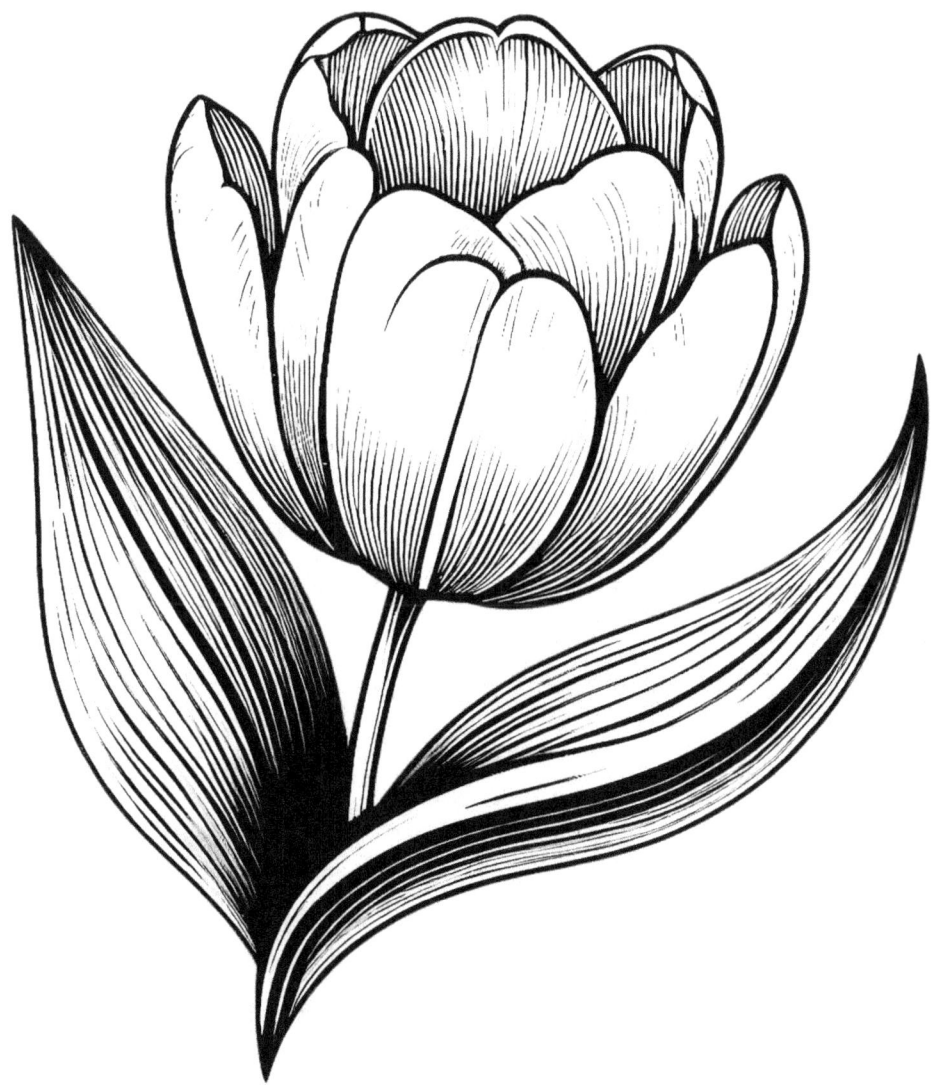

Elegant and vibrant, tulips symbolize love and springtime, available in a variety of colors.

Zinnia

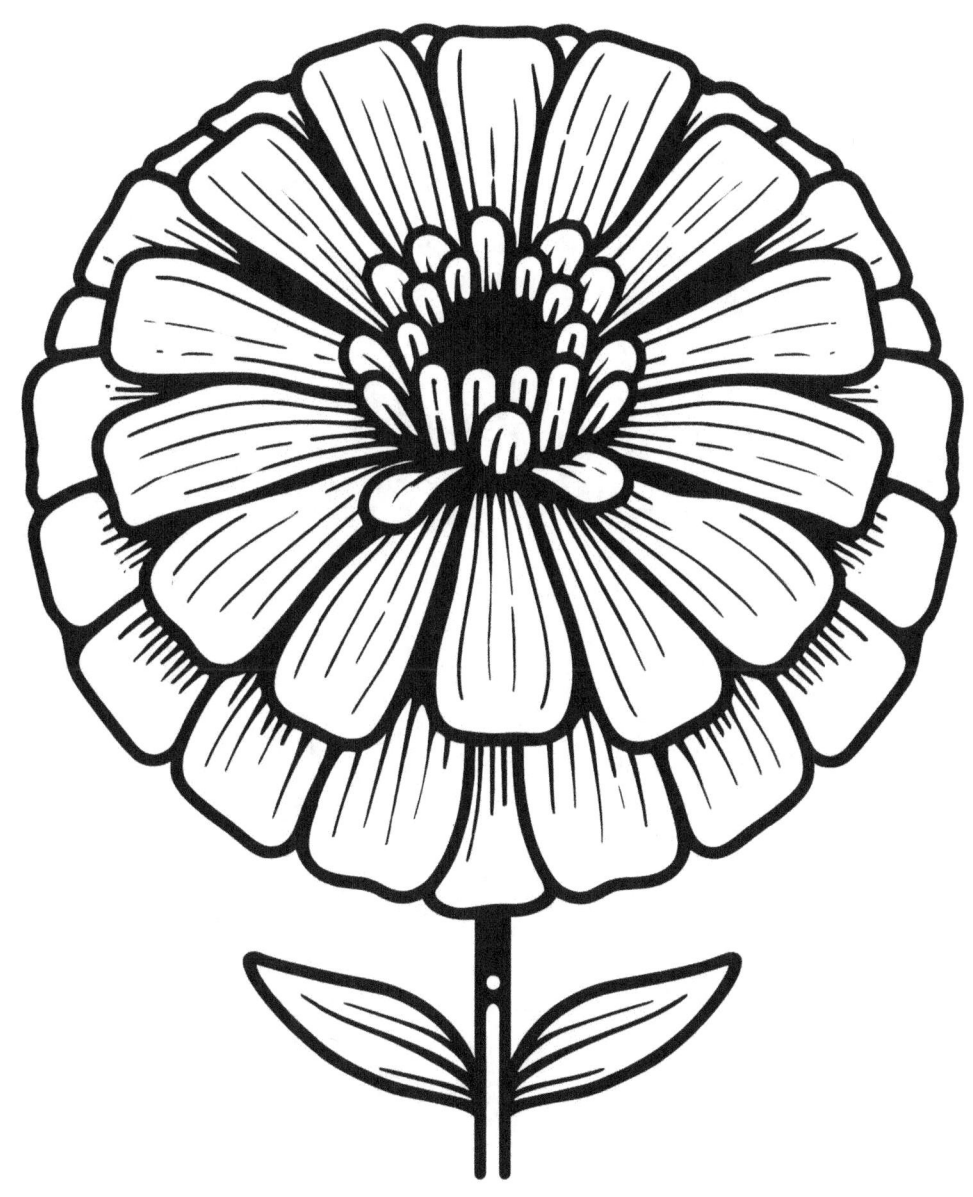

Zinnias are colorful and easy-to-grow flowers, symbolizing endurance, constancy, and lasting friendship.

Ranunculus

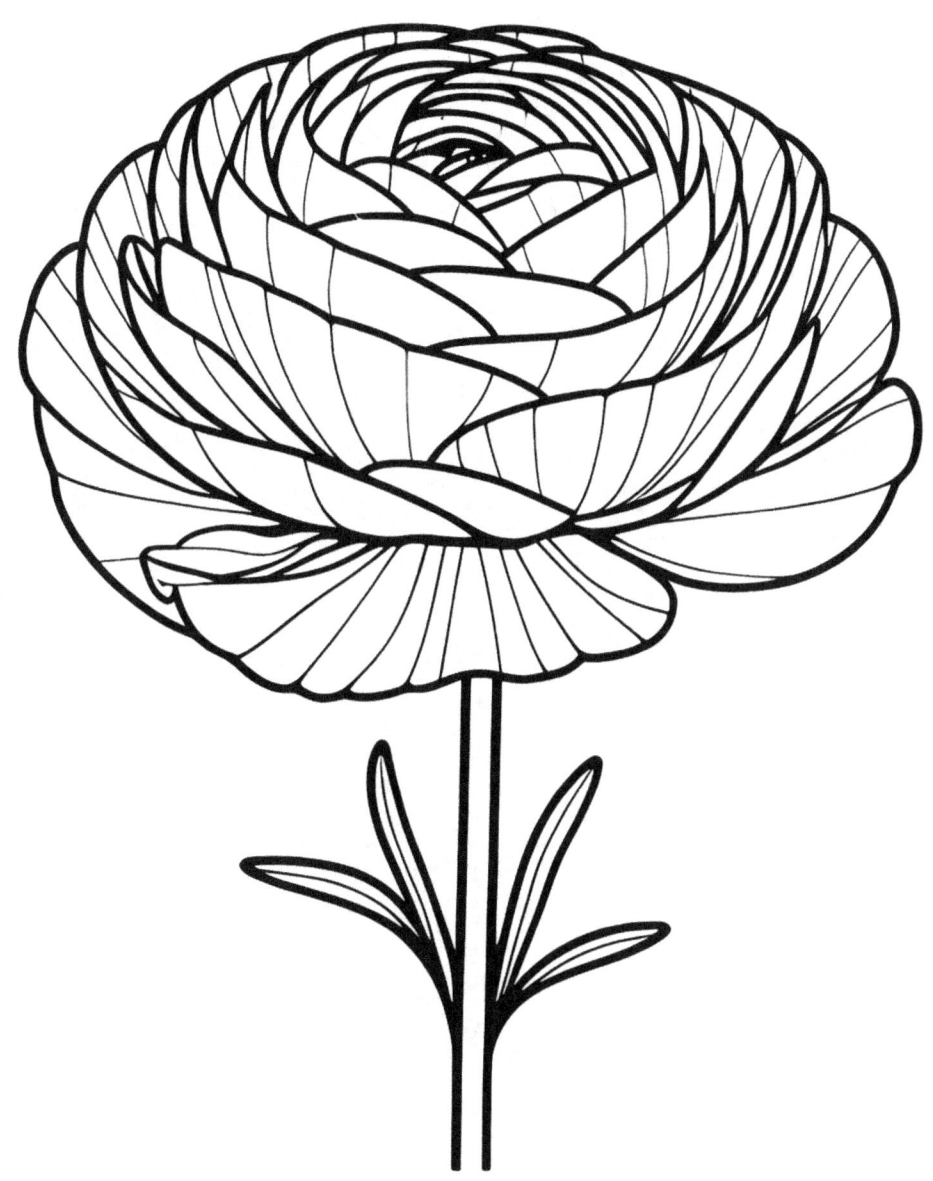

Ranunculus flowers are prized for their delicate petals and vibrant colors, symbolizing charm and attractiveness.

Poppy

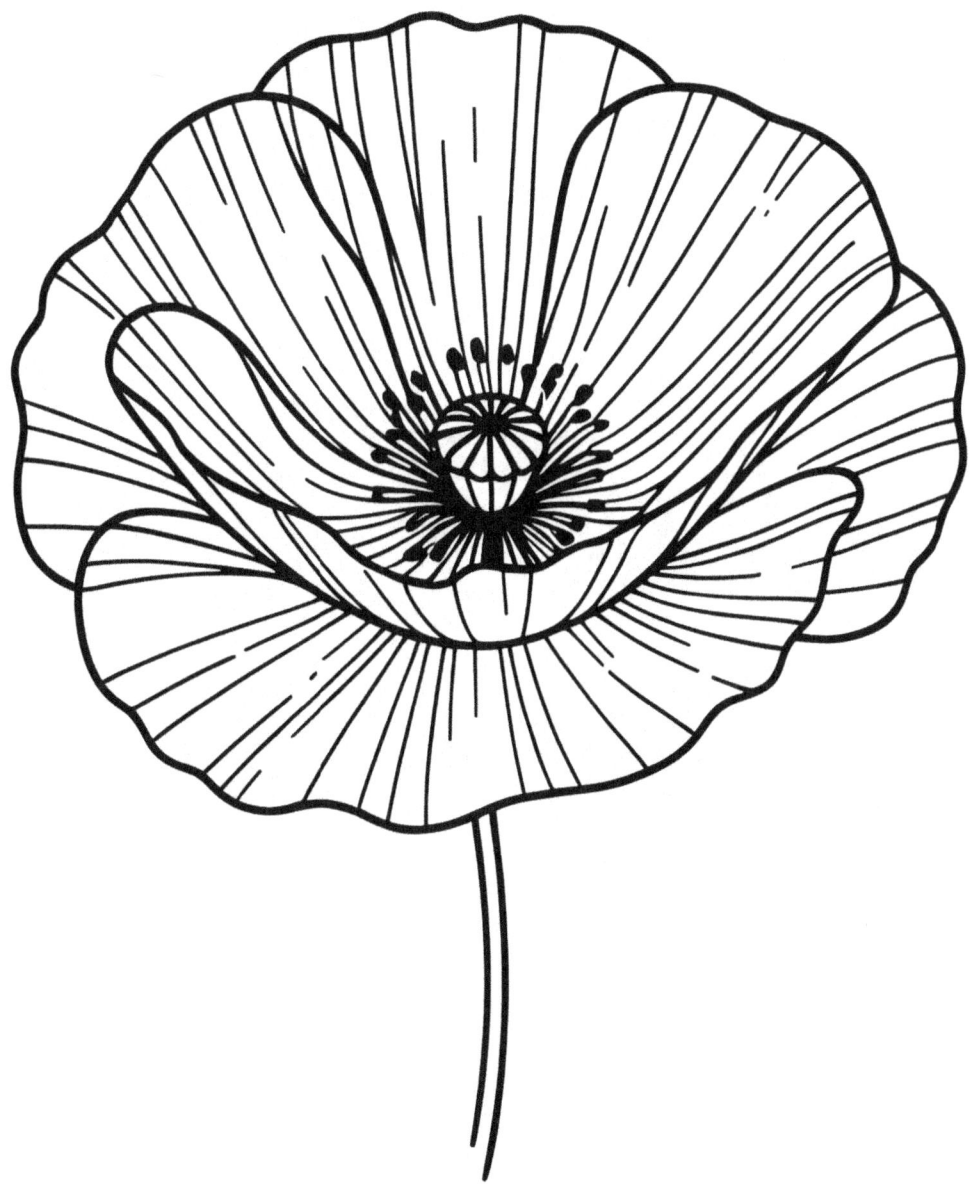

Poppies are bold and vibrant flowers that symbolize remembrance, consolation, and imagination.

Aster

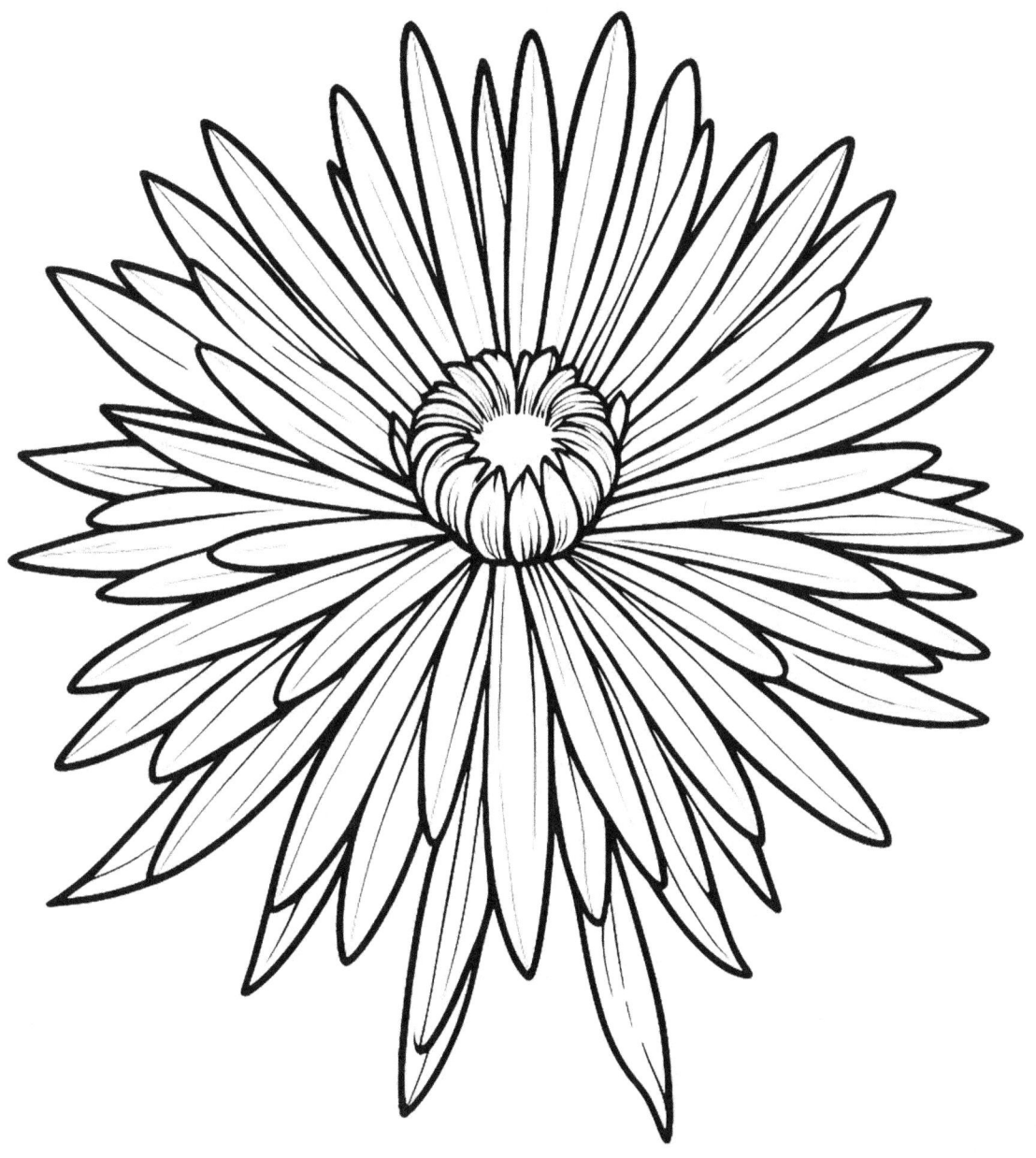

Aster flowers have star-shaped blooms and symbolize love, patience, and elegance.

Cosmos

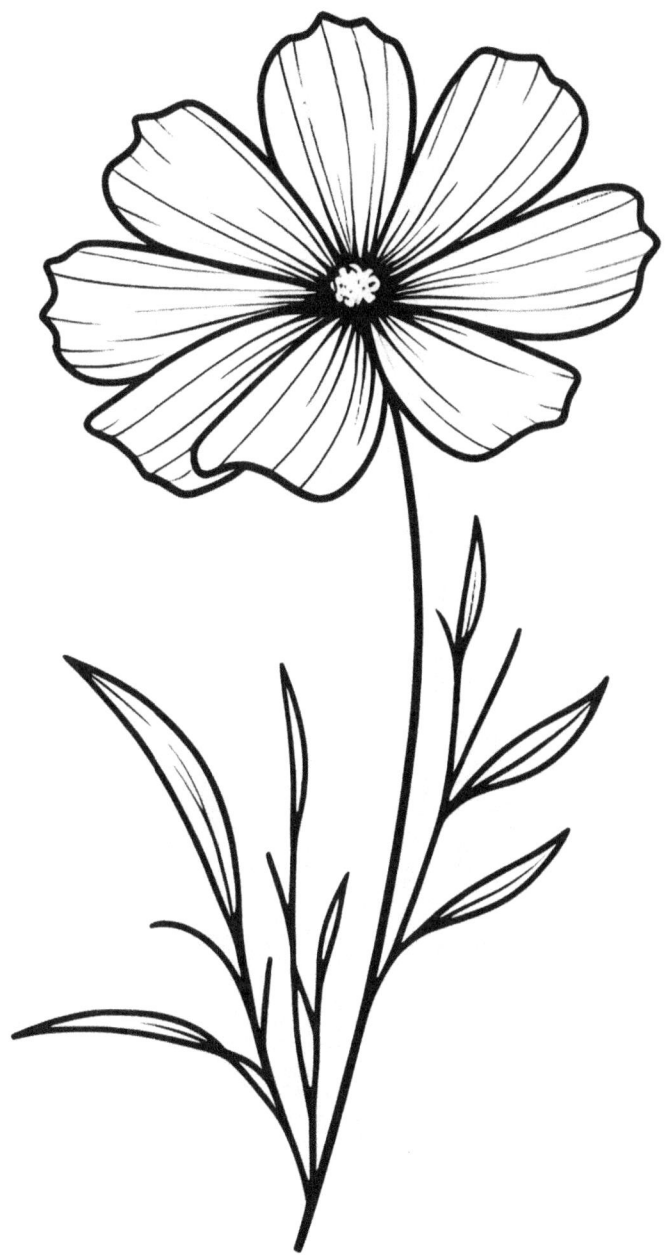

Cosmos flowers have delicate, daisy-like blooms and symbolize peace, harmony, and order.

Anemone

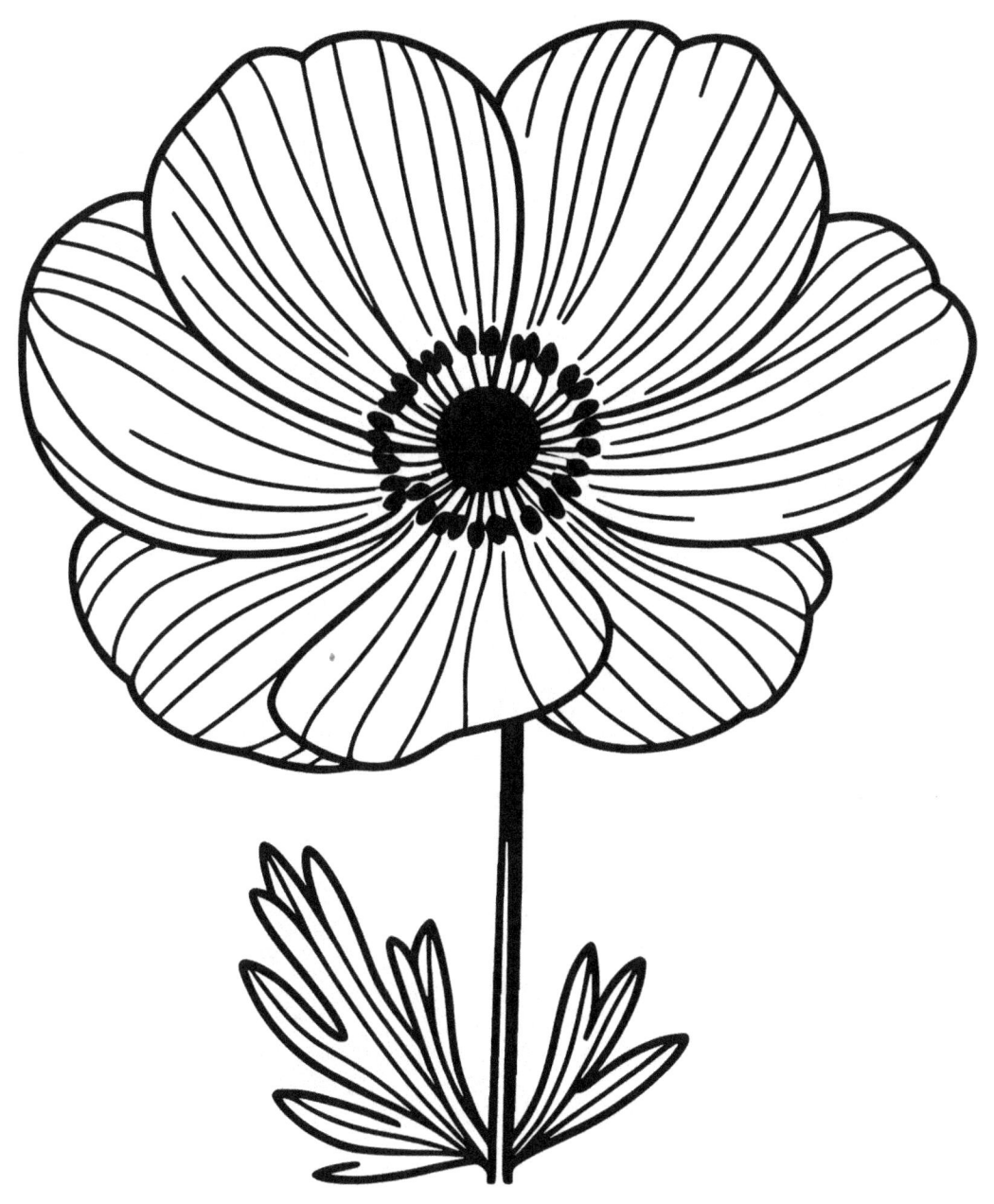

Anemone flowers come in various colors and symbolize anticipation, protection, and luck.

Gladiolus

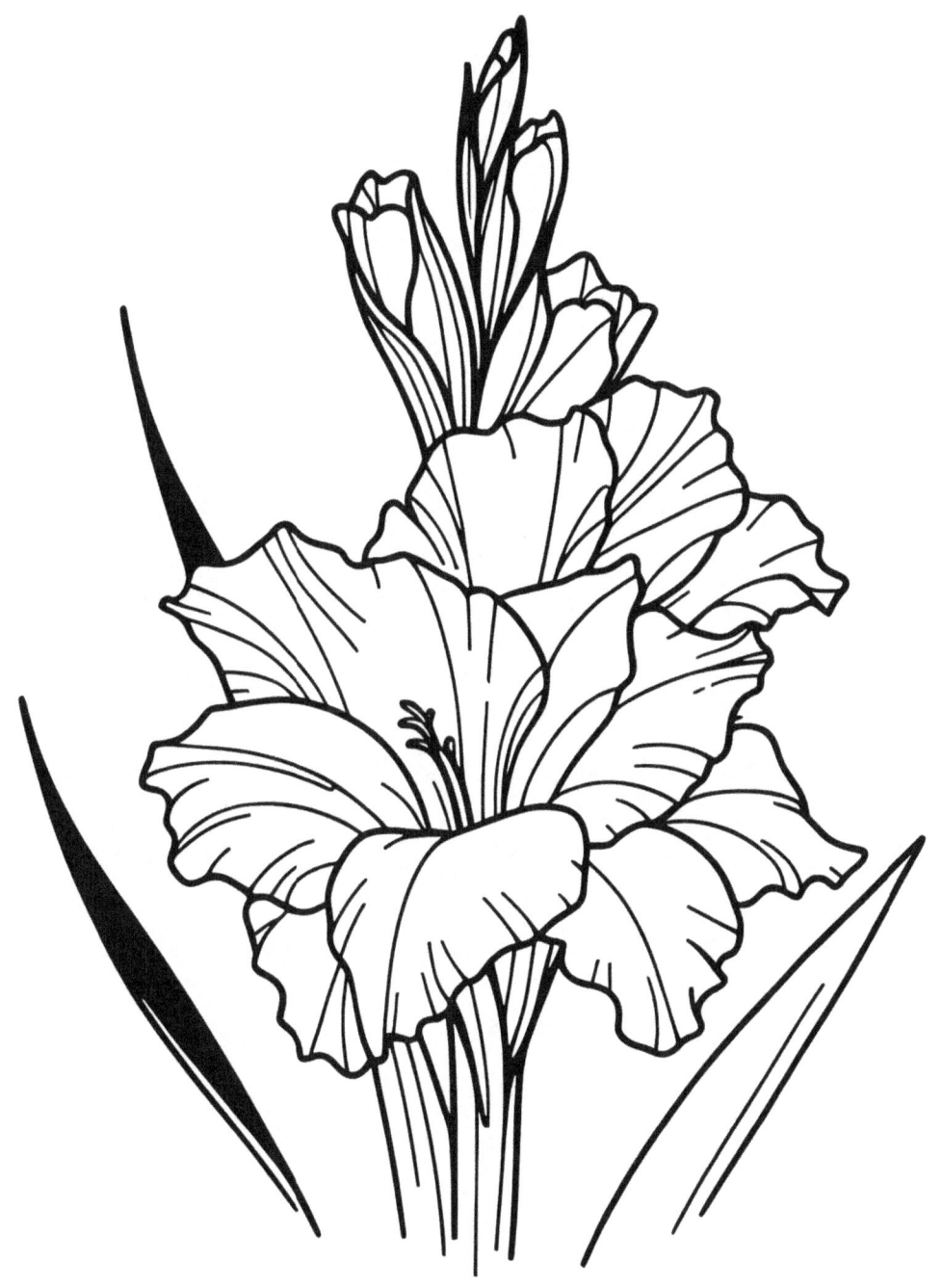

Gladiolus flowers are tall and elegant, symbolizing strength of character, sincerity, and remembrance.

Lily of the Valley

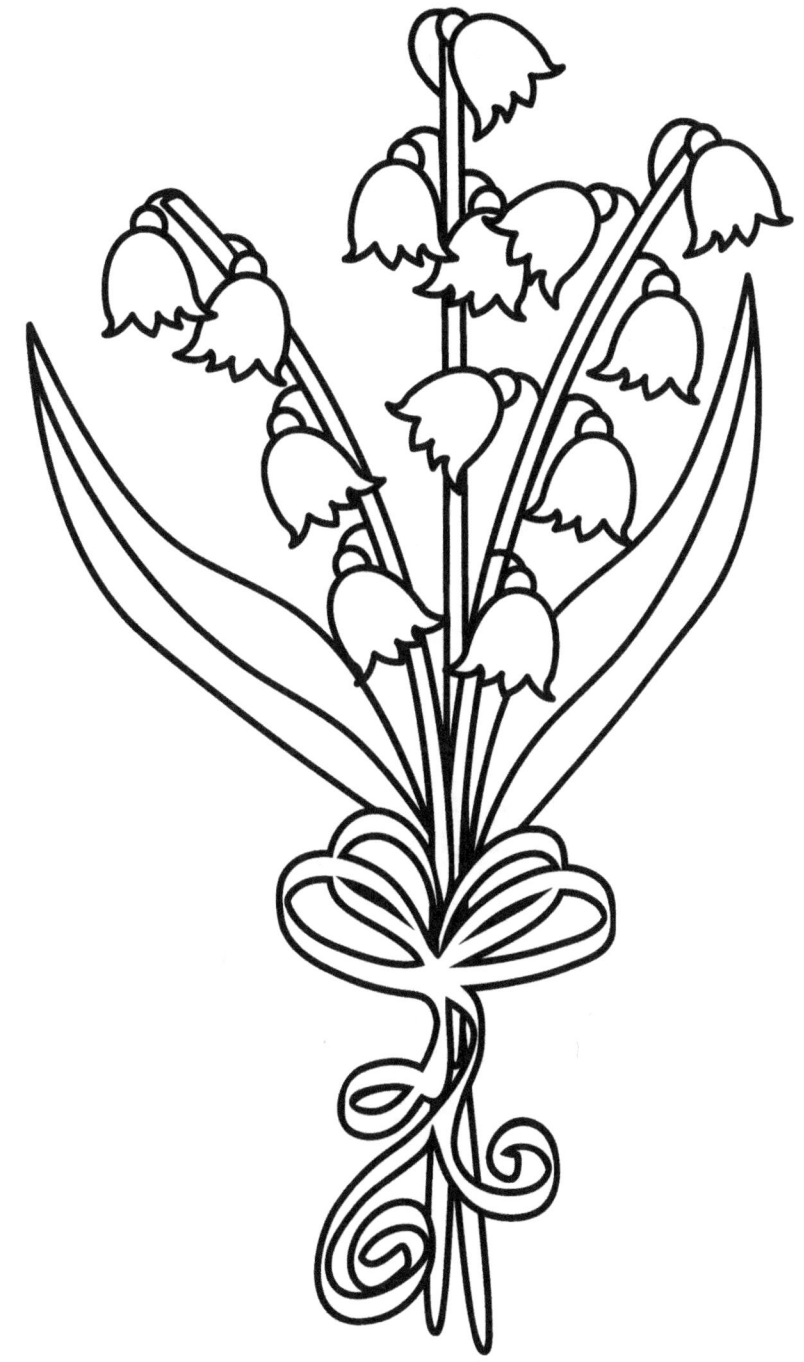

Delicate and fragrant, lily of the valley symbolizes sweetness, purity, and happiness.

Hyacinth

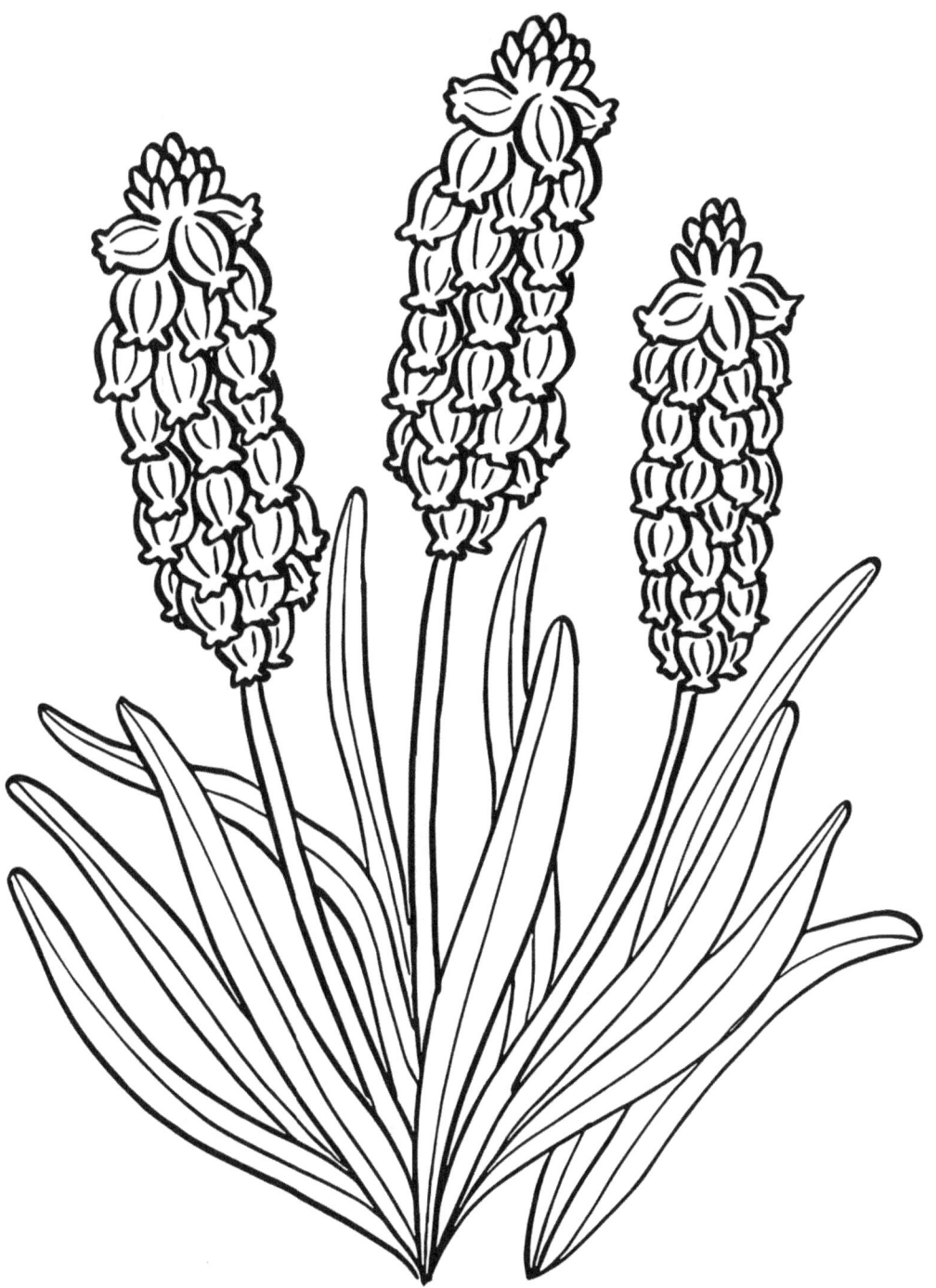

Hyacinths are fragrant spring flowers that symbolize sincerity, constancy, and sincerity.

Bird of Paradise

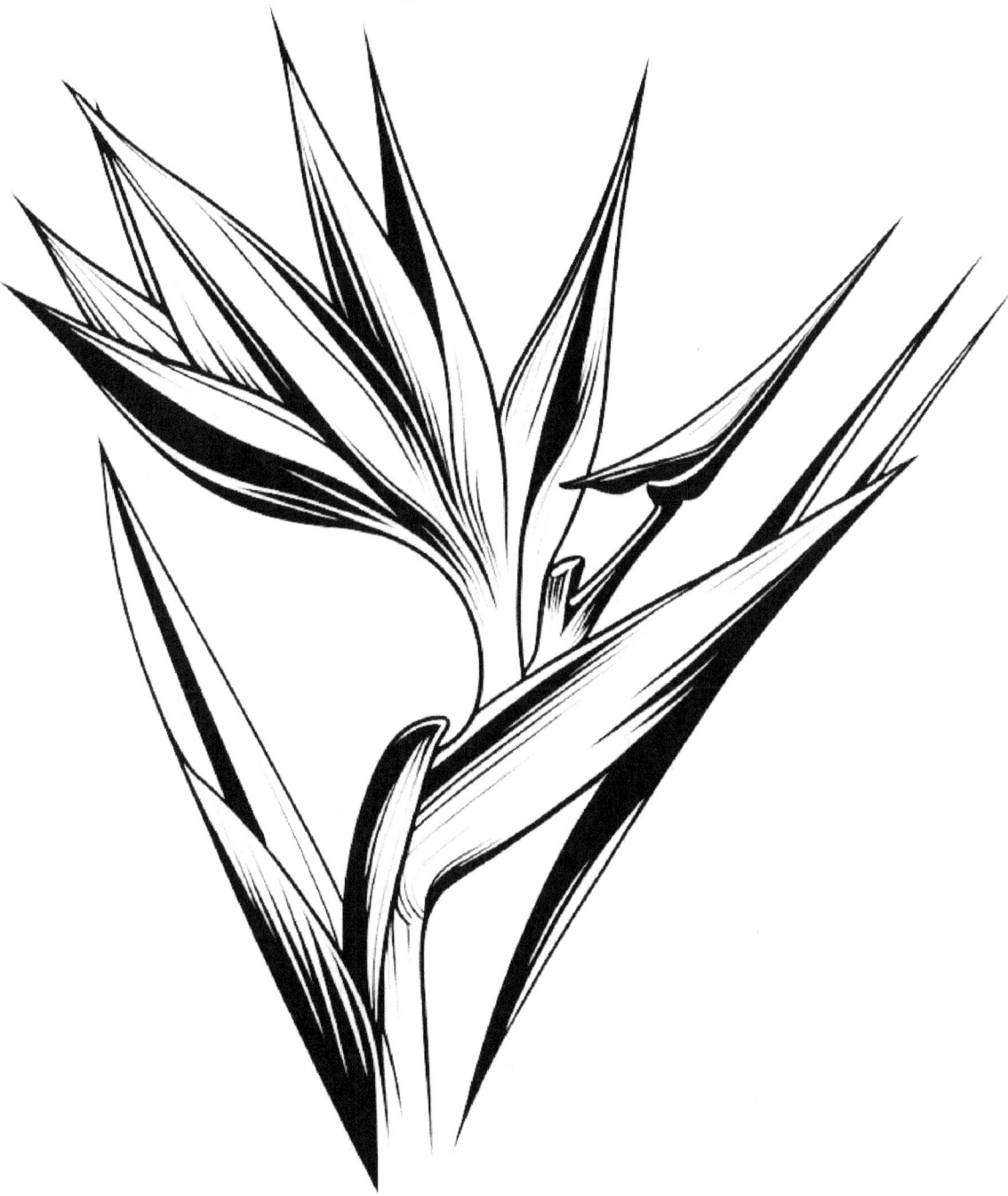

Exotic and striking, bird of paradise flowers symbolize freedom, joy, and paradise.

Dahlia

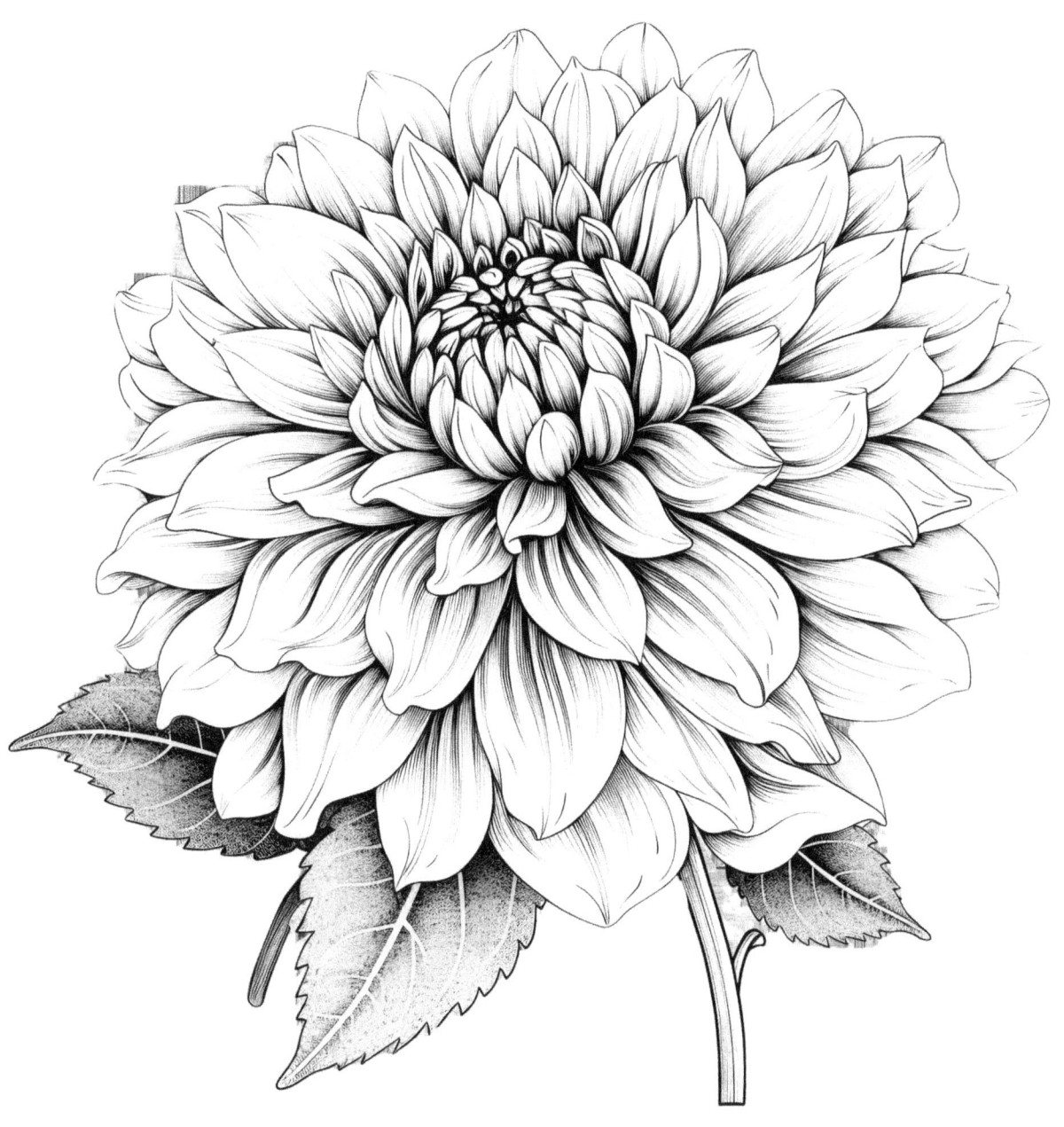

Dahlias come in various shapes and sizes, symbolizing elegance, inner strength, and creativity.

Freesia

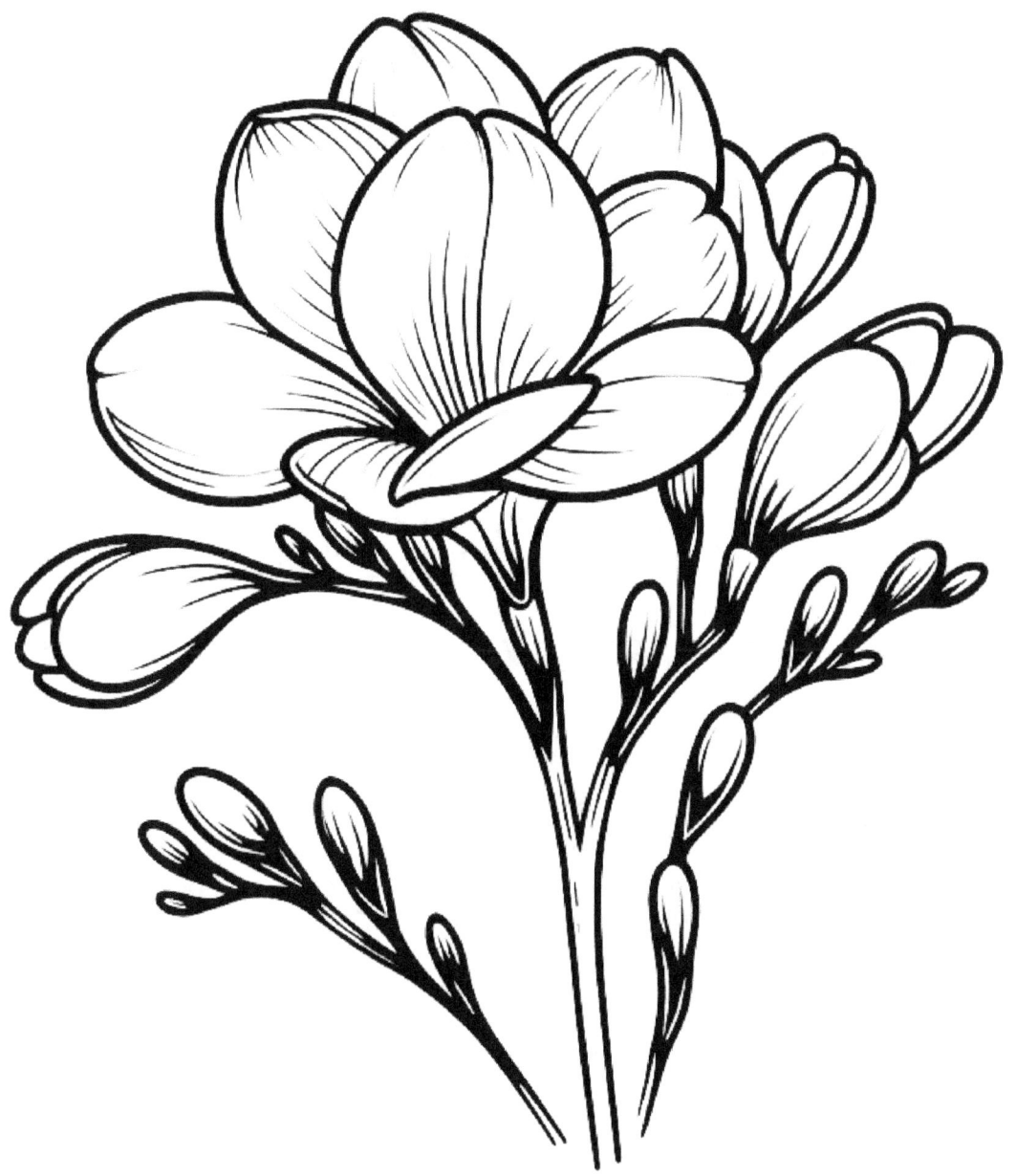

Freesias are fragrant flowers that symbolize innocence, thoughtfulness, and friendship.

Sweet Pea

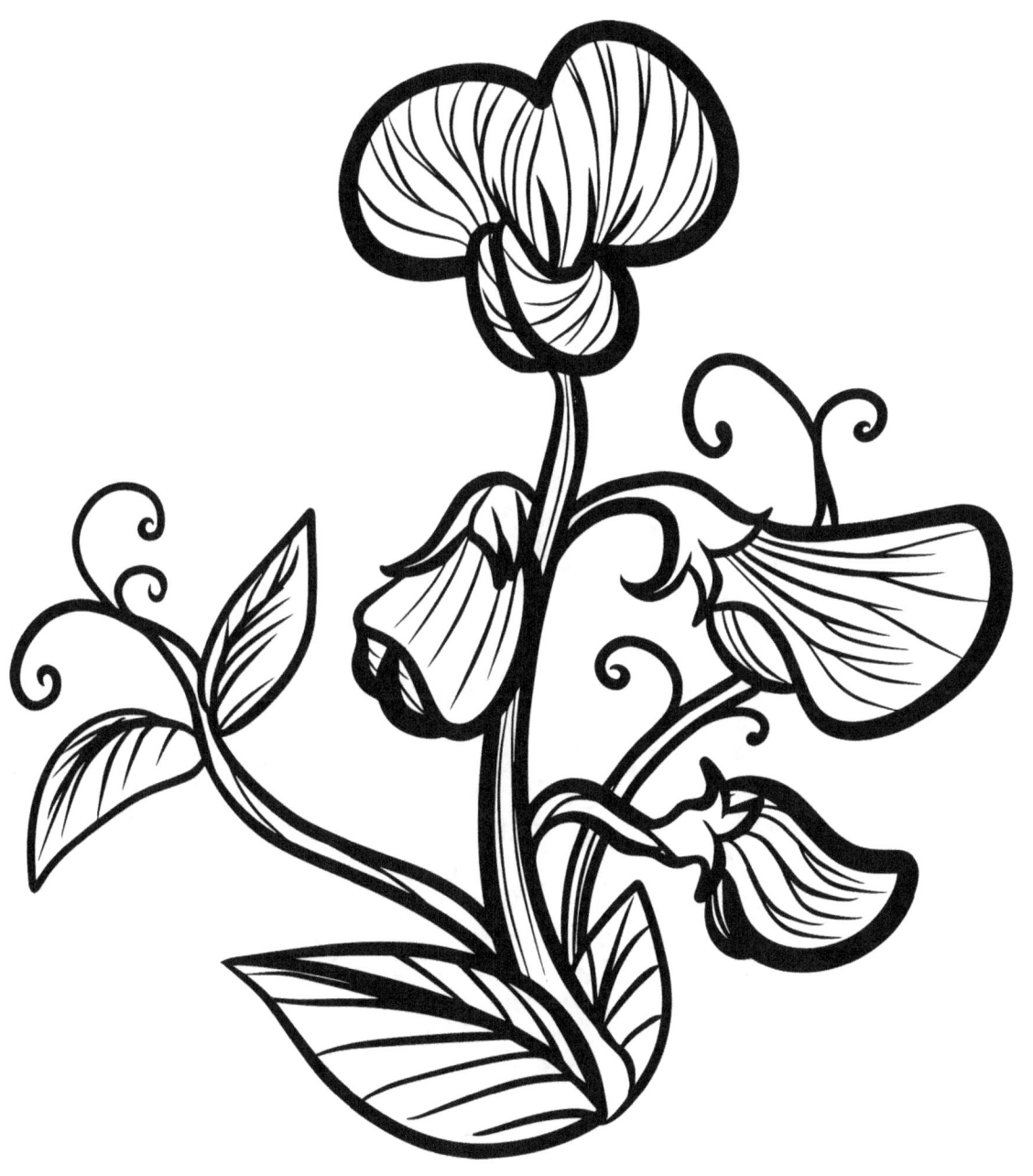

Sweet peas are fragrant flowers that symbolize blissful pleasure, gratitude, and delicate pleasures.

Geranium

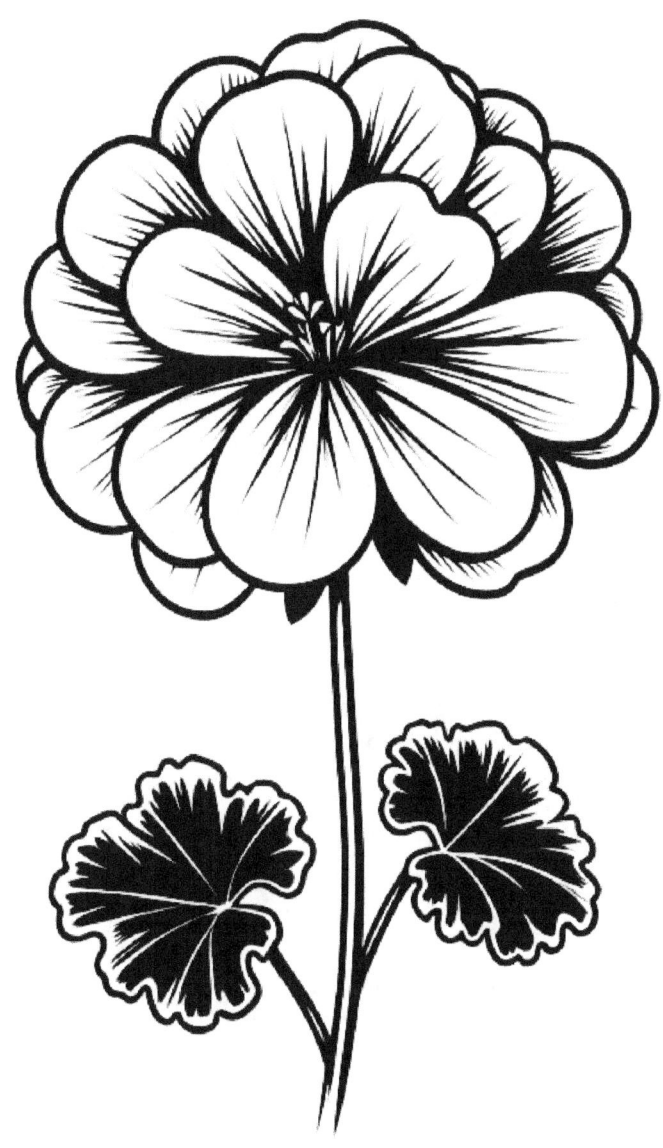

Geraniums are popular bedding plants with colorful blooms and symbolize friendship and comfort.

Lisianthus

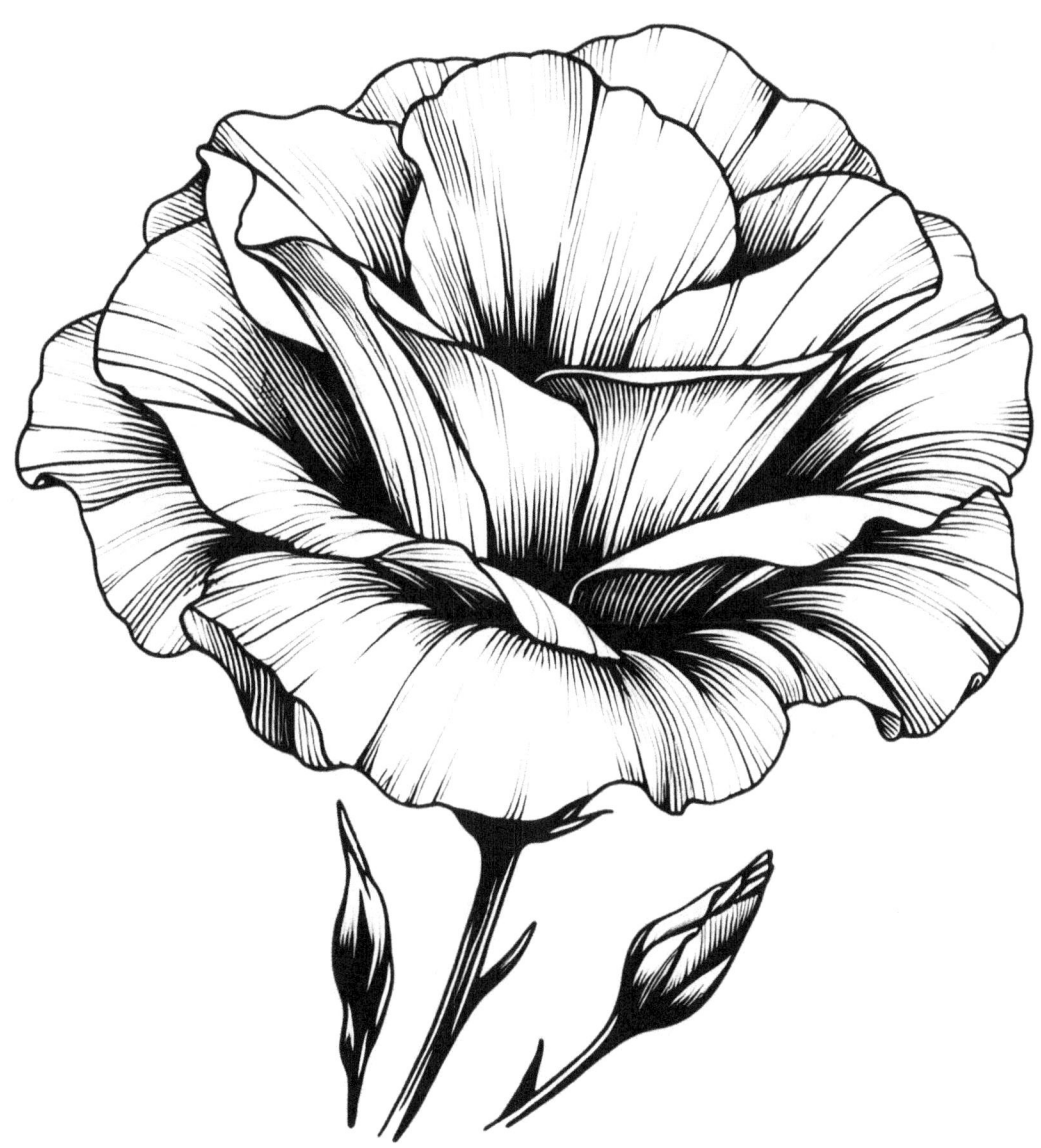

Lisianthus flowers have delicate, rose-like blooms and symbolize appreciation, charisma, and grace.

Nasturtium

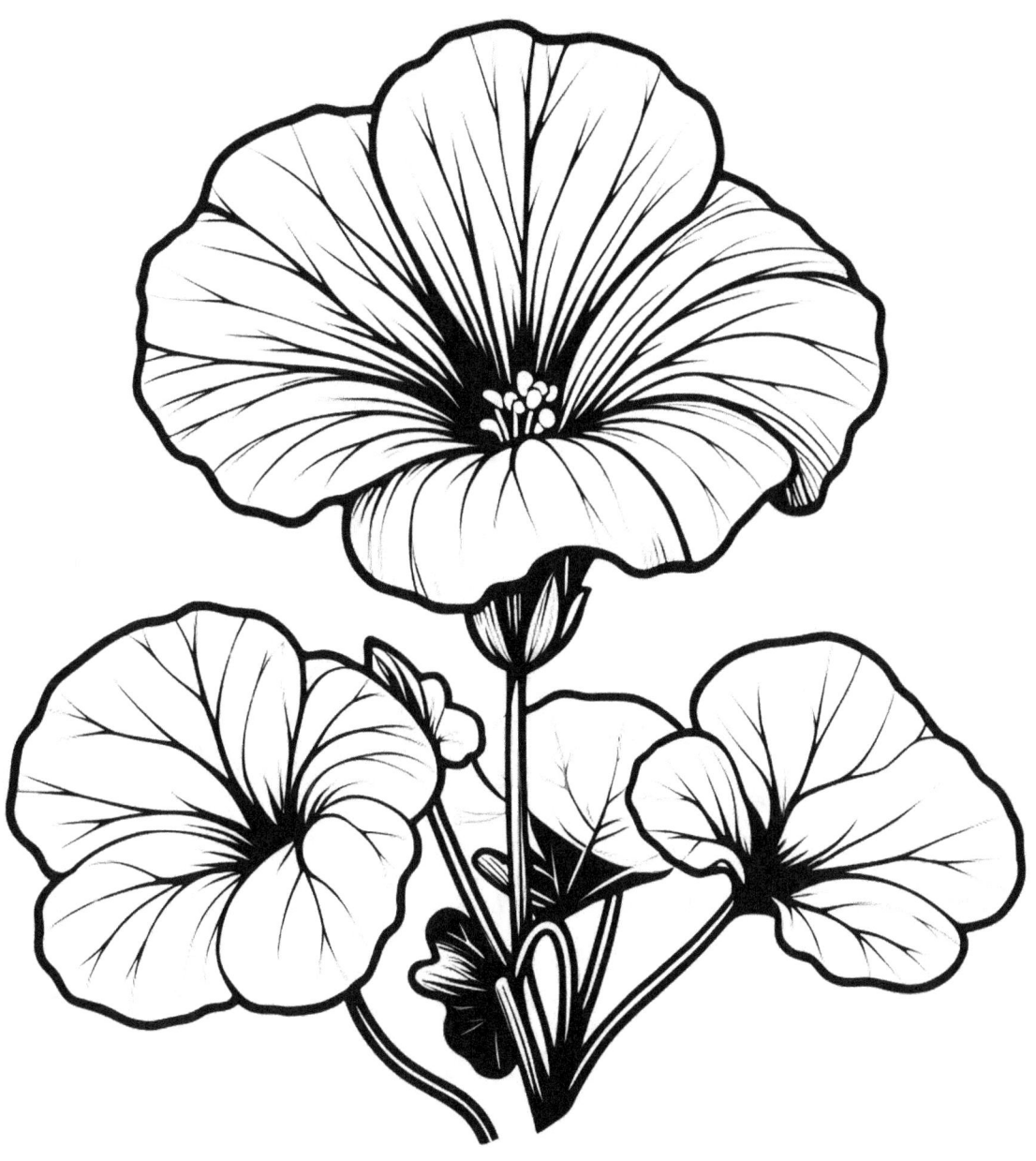

Nasturtium flowers come in vibrant colors and symbolize victory in battle, conquest, and patriotism.

Verbena

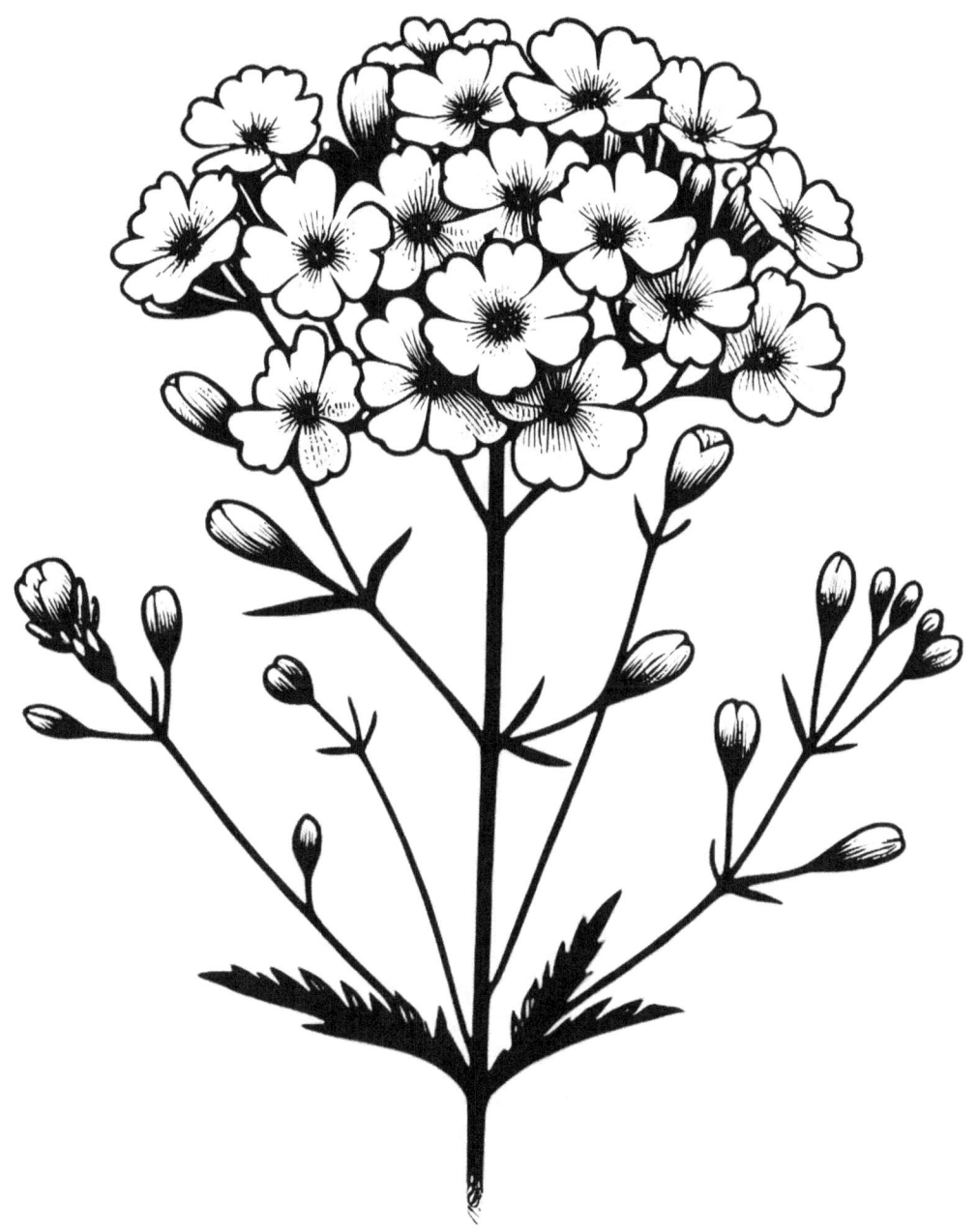

Verbena flowers are drought-tolerant and symbolize healing, creativity, and magical protection.

Pansy

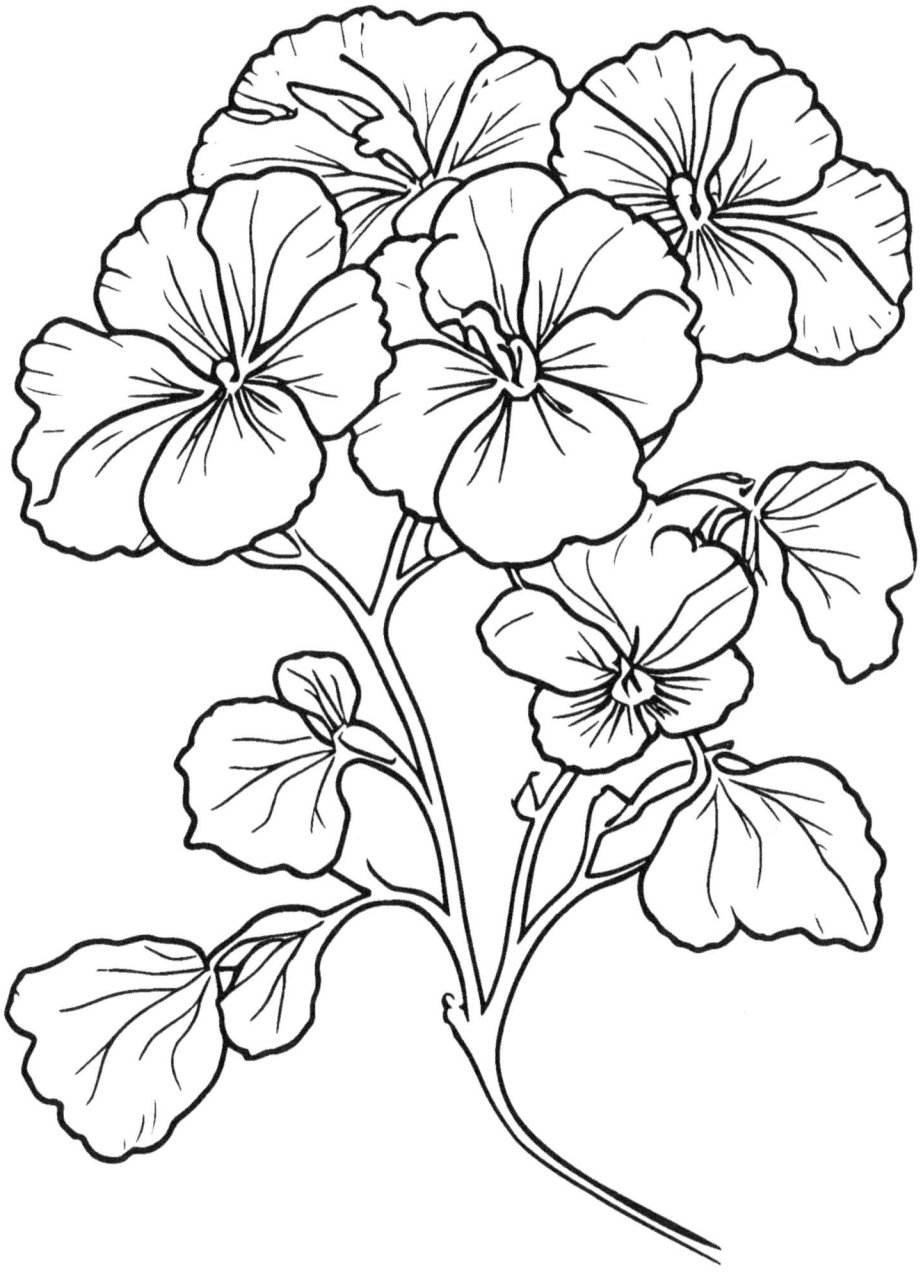

Pansies are colorful flowers with "faces" and symbolize thoughtfulness, remembrance, and affection.

Canterbury Bells

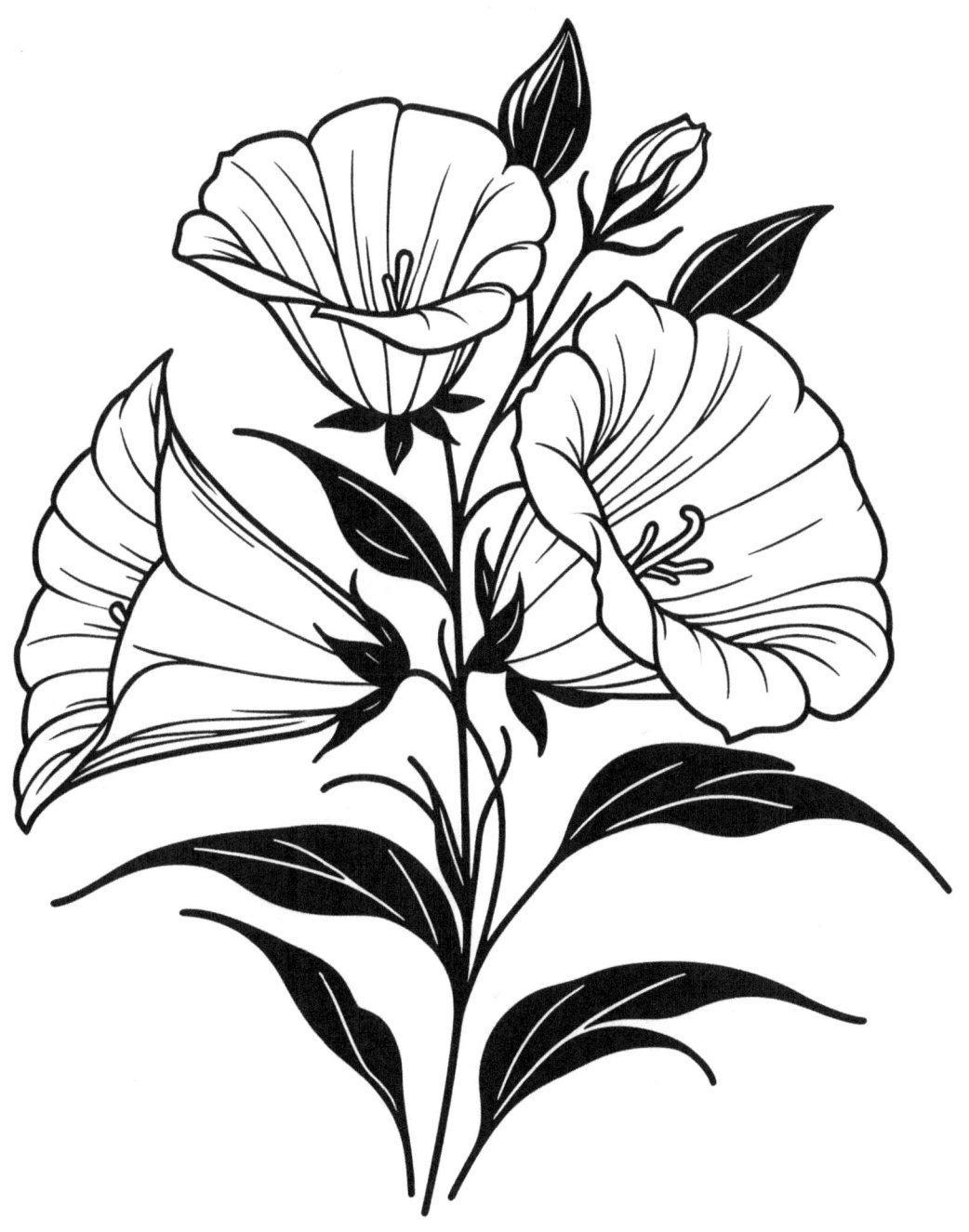

Canterbury bells are bell-shaped flowers that symbolize gratitude, faith, and constancy.

Foxglove

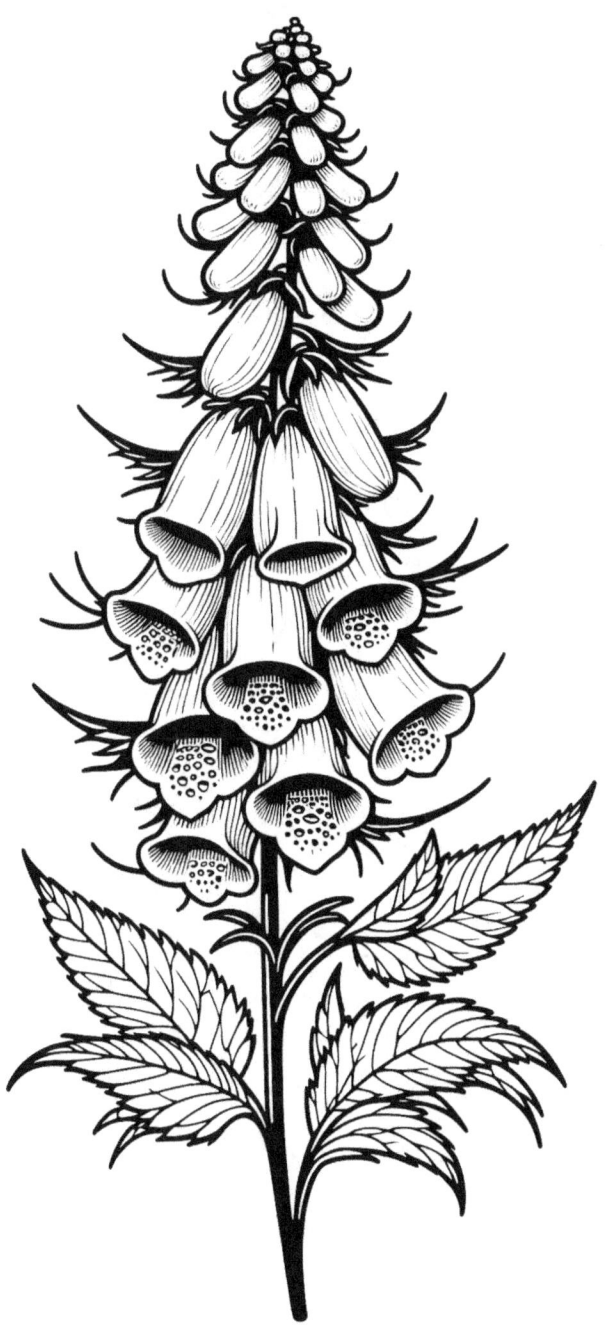

Foxglove flowers have tall spires of tubular blooms and symbolize insincerity, ambition, and creativity.

Hollyhock

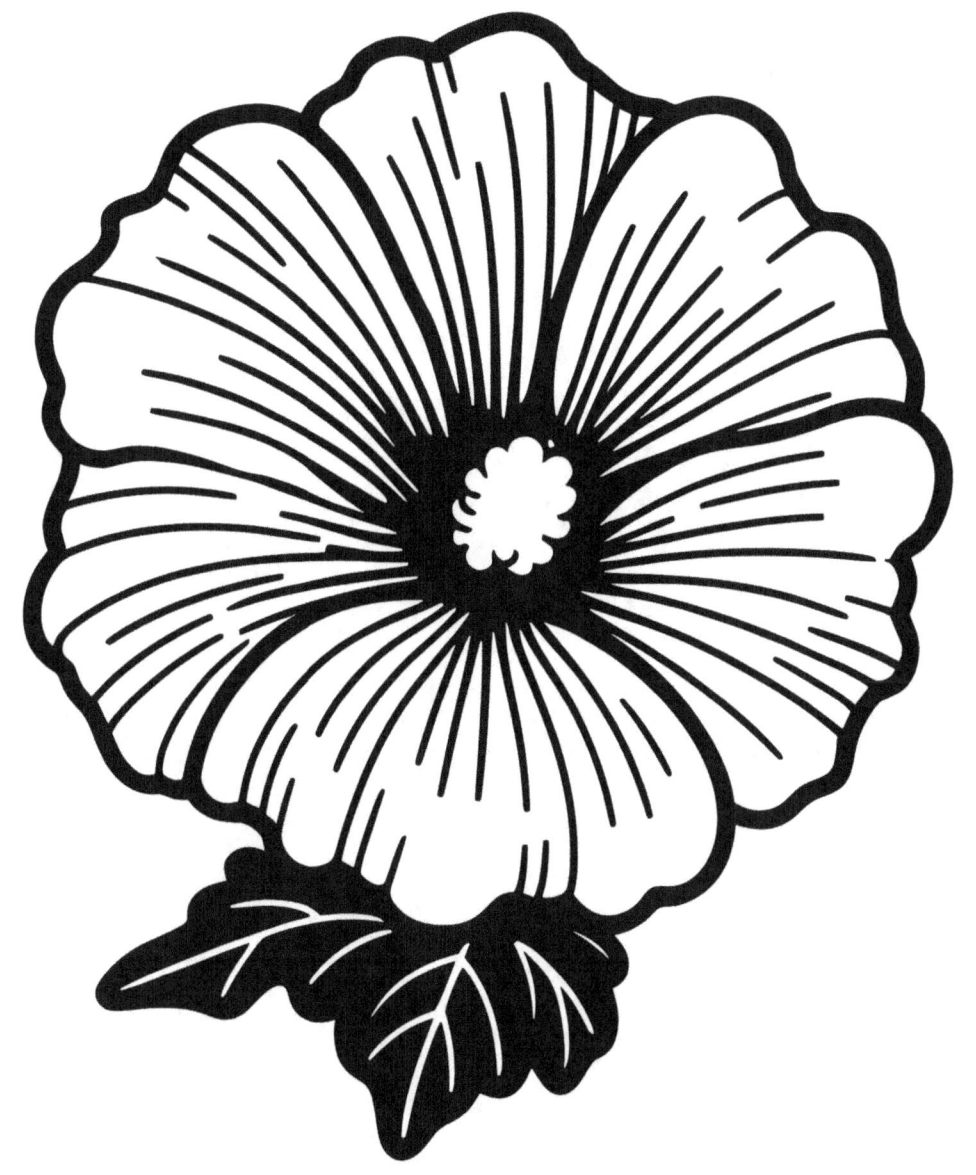

Hollyhocks are tall, stately flowers that symbolize fertility, abundance, and growth.

Gardenia

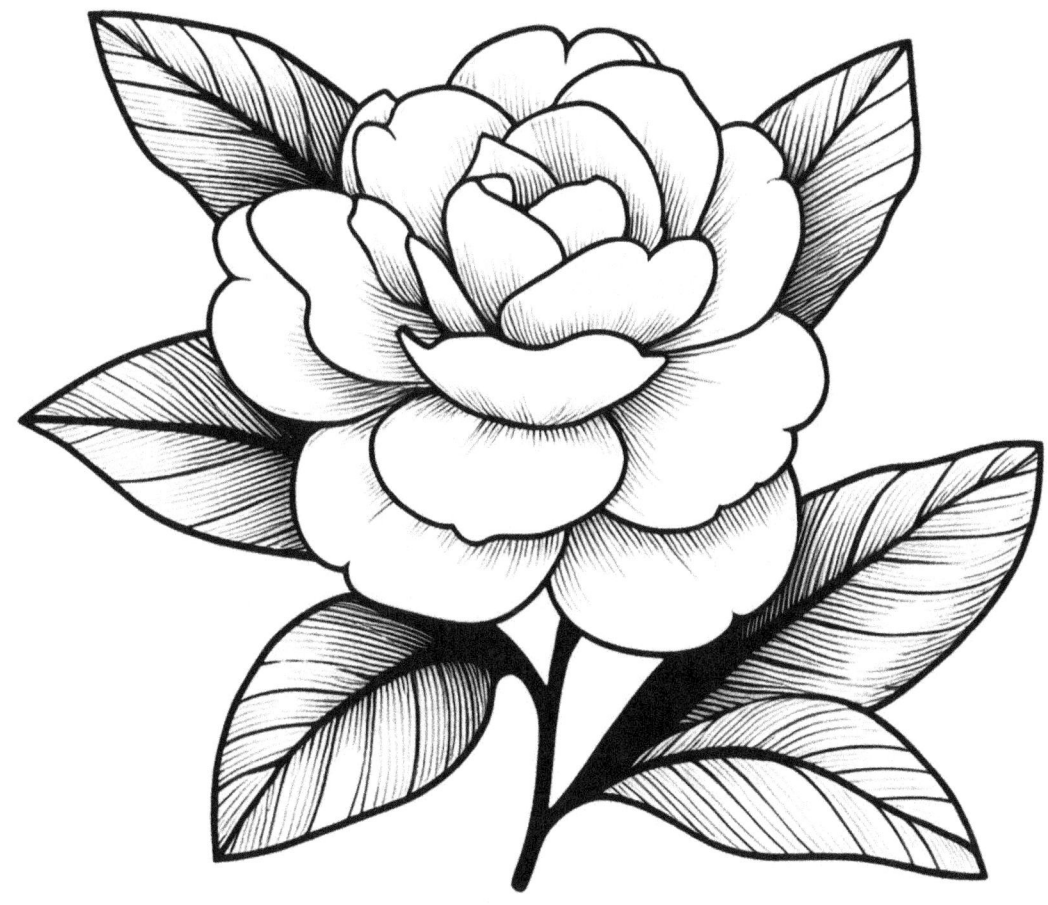

Gardenias are known for their beautiful white blooms and intoxicating fragrance. They symbolize purity and sweetness. Their creamy white petals and glossy, dark green leaves make them a favorite in gardens and as cut flowers in floral arrangements.

Begonia

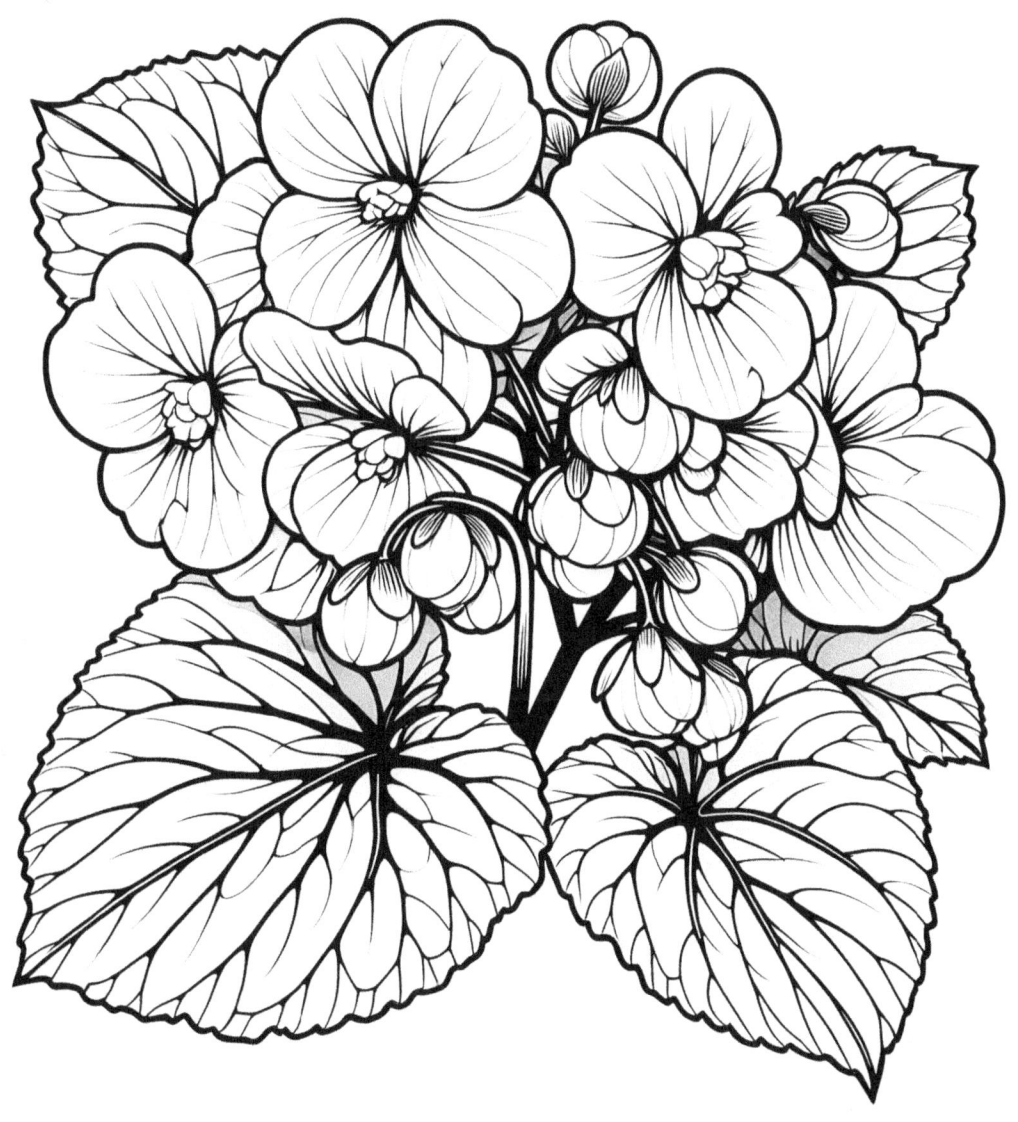

Begonias are versatile, colorful flowers with a wide variety of appearances. Begonias symbolize caution, a deep thought process, and individuality due to their many unique shapes and colors.

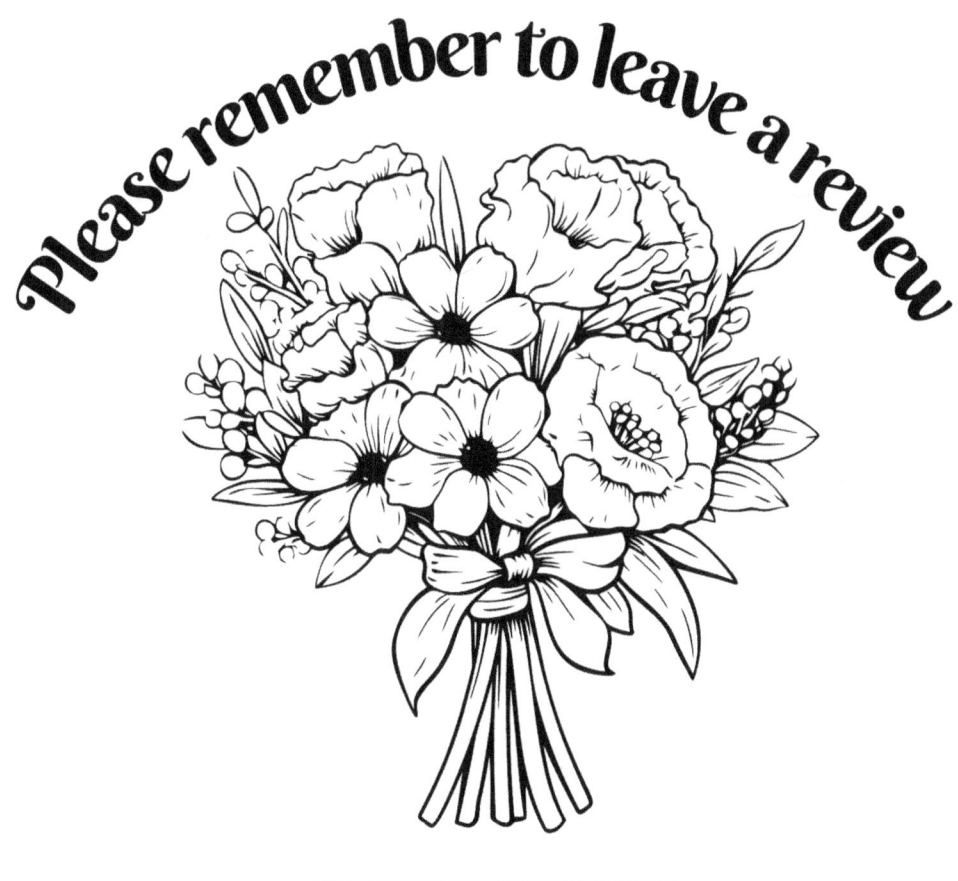

Please remember to leave a review

OR VISIT:
https://www.cascadiawavemedia.com/review.php?book=B0D2VK42QC

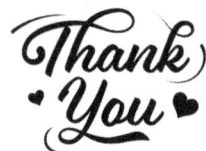

www.ingramcontent.com/pod-product-compliance
Lightning Source LLC
Chambersburg PA
CBHW062226220526
45471CB00009B/3360